PARADISE ON·THE HUDSON

PARADISE ON THE HUDSON

The CREATION, LOSS, and REVIVAL of a GREAT AMERICAN GARDEN

CAROLINE SEEBOHM

TIMBER PRESS
Portland, Oregon

Frontispiece: The Temple of Love at Untermyer Gardens has a prime view across the Hudson River, to fall colors and the cliffs of the Palisades. Opposite: Hosta blooms and variegated Japanese forest grass are favorites in the restored garden.

Photography and illustration credits begin on page 211.

Published in 2020 by Timber Press, Inc.
The Haseltine Building
133 S.W. Second Avenue, Suite 450
Portland, OR 97204-3527
timberpress.com

Printed in China
Cover design by Raphael Geroni
Text design by Sarah Crumb

ISBN 978-1-60469-857-2
Catalog records for this book are available from the Library of Congress and the British Library.

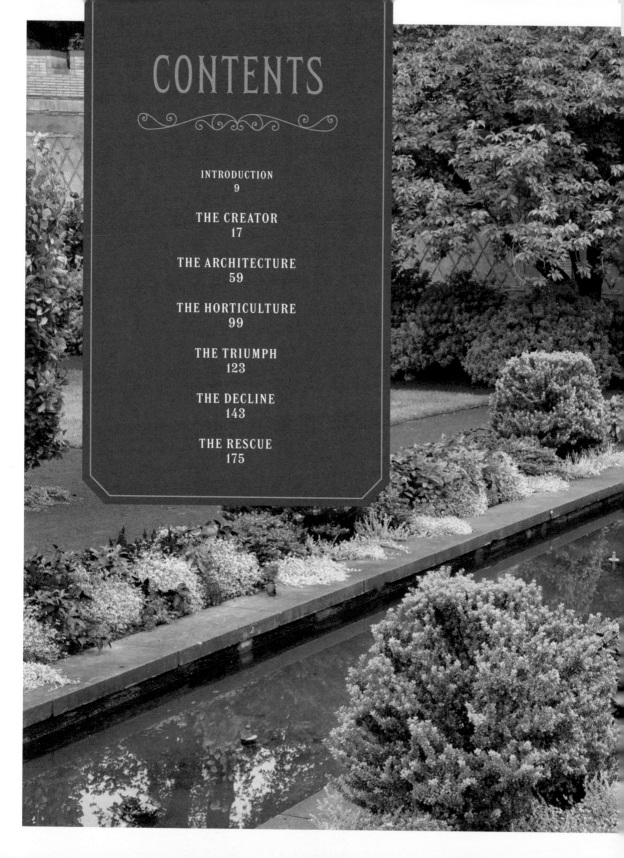

CONTENTS

A main axis canal runs north-south in the Walled Garden, ending on the north end with the sphinxes and the amphitheater. The circular Temple of the Sky is to the west (left).

INTRODUCTION

In the early morning, with the mist rolling up from the river, you might think you have come upon the ruins of an ancient civilization: tall white pillars, Greek temples, a walled garden, an amphitheater, Moorish-style canals, stone-carved sphinxes, Chinese-like rock formations, twisting paths, crumbling walls, and a long staircase unfolding in a seemingly endless pale ribbon down to the water. Like a ghostly vision of paradise, the garden emerges, revealing everything and nothing. It seems unable—yet—to tell its secret.

This is the story of the making of that garden, and the man behind it. Both remain somewhat enigmatic to this day, extraordinary as it may seem in a time when so much information is at our fingertips. It harks back to different, more flamboyant times, and yet how reassuring it is in its confirmation of the power of the human spirit.

The garden came into being on the banks of the Hudson River, in Yonkers, New York. It was the brainchild of a brilliant, contentious millionaire, a Zionist Jew who married a Christian, a man who was a supporter of women's suffrage, a partner in the first and most successful Jewish law firm in New York, who advocated unpopular legal and financial reforms,

Samuel Untermyer: ambitious, successful,
and orchid-adorned New York attorney.

and who very early foresaw the threat of Hitler. Married to a lover of art
and music (his wife helped bring Gustav Mahler to New York), friend and
supporter of Albert Einstein, this Democratic Party activist and celebrity
lawyer also dreamed of creating a landscape that would bring the worlds of
art, architecture, music, and horticulture together for the enjoyment of all.

His name was Samuel Untermyer.

Who knows about this extraordinary New Yorker? His name is not
in the pantheon of early twentieth-century titans such as Rockefeller,
Morgan, or Carnegie; not inscribed on any library, hospital, or art museum
in the city. Only a small fountain in Central Park's Conservatory Garden

in New York bears his name. Yet his career touched on many of the great issues of the day, and he knew most of the major figures in local and national politics from the 1890s until his death in 1940.

Untermyer cultivated a fierce, take-no-prisoners technique that was generally put to use in support of progressive causes, including bank regulation and real estate racketeering. His clients included Hapsburgs, Ottoman sultans, ambassadors, movie moguls, newspaper barons, and celebrities.

The only idiosyncratic aspect of this fearsome man was his habit of wearing a fresh odontioda orchid in his buttonhole every day to court. Uncharacteristic, surely. A clue? Perhaps. For a completely different accomplishment plucked Samuel Untermyer out of this cutthroat world of social, legal, and political activism, immortalizing his name in another sphere entirely.

In 1899, Untermyer acquired Greystone, a turreted mansion and vast estate on the banks of the Hudson River. Like most wealthy property owners of the time, he envisaged a garden, and in 1916 he chose William Welles Bosworth to design it for him. Bosworth was a famous architect who had worked at Kykuit, the Rockefellers' grand estate in Pocantico Hills, New York. Competitive as always, Untermyer demanded "the finest garden in the world." Bosworth took his client at his word.

The result was beyond anyone's wildest dreams. The design grew out of a vision of the Garden of Eden as described in the Book of Genesis. A walled garden was the first requirement, inspired by the great Persian and Islamic enclosed water gardens of the eighth to fifteenth centuries. Long canals represented the four ancient rivers, punctuated by small fountains and meeting at four central intersections. Octagonal towers marked the corners of the garden. An amphitheater dominated the far end, guarded by two sphinxes carved by Paul Manship, the premier American sculptor of the time. Overlooking the sweep of land going down to the river stood a Greek tempietto. In front of that, a swimming pool and lower terrace were decorated with ornamental tiles and mosaics.

The Temple of Love, a popular feature of Untermyer Gardens.

Leading away from the amphitheater, a modest doorway invited visitors to embark upon a spectacularly long and wide staircase down to the Hudson River. Two ancient and monolithic pillars framed the dramatic finale of the vista overlooking the Palisades, a twenty-mile stretch of exposed, steep cliffs on the west side of the Hudson River

Untermyer was a passionate plantsman, and Bosworth saw to it that his client's botanical desires were satisfied. Flower gardens were planted in the northern part of the landscape, each with a single color—quite revolutionary at a time when English-style, multicolored herbaceous borders were all the rage. Vegetable gardens and flowers shaded by pavilions flourished in beds and arbors farther down the slope toward the river bank.

No respectable garden at that time was complete without a folly, and Bosworth devised a delicate, Greek-style feature that was called the Temple of Love, sited at the top of a dizzying "mount" of rock formations, not unlike the naturally formed limestone rocks characteristic of early Chinese gardens. Waterfalls cascaded down these rocks into a pool below, the sound and movement creating a kind of *son et lumière* to encompass the fragile temple at the top. What Untermyer and his architect achieved was the most original garden landscape in America: a meeting place of differing cultures and beliefs, reflected in the themes of Persia, India, Greece, and Italy. It was a paradise of harmony in a world that sorely needed it.

To that end, Untermyer had always intended that the gardens be enjoyed, not just by his family and friends, but by the American people. And the people came—flocks of them, from all over—rich and poor, famous and infamous. Isadora Duncan danced there. Celebrated musicians played there. Artists were inspired there. Untermyer, the lion of the courtroom, had created a wonderland. That ever-present odontioda orchid had perhaps been a clue after all.

For about twenty-five years, the garden flourished. On a single day in September 1939, 30,000 visitors were reported to have made their way to Yonkers to see what Untermyer had wrought along the steep slopes of the Hudson. As records were being broken at the Untermyer gardens, however, halfway across several continents, World War II was looming. As early as 1933, Untermyer had sensed the dangers of Germany's Third Reich, speaking out for boycotts and publishing speeches against Nazism so effectively that the British press called him "Hitler's Bitterest Foe." In 1940, shortly before the European conflict plunged the United States into war, Samuel Untermyer died in Palm Springs at the age of 82. Perhaps he was fortunate to go at that moment, before he could witness the horrors that unfolded in spite of his warnings.

Untermyer had hoped his Yonkers house and garden would become a state park after his death, but he failed to provide an endowment. Neither New York State nor Westchester County was willing or able to assume

A simple doorway leads to the Vista.

the burden of Untermyer's celebrated property, particularly since the war was threatening lives across the country. It was no time for even small sums of money to be invested in trivial projects like a rich man's garden. In 1946, some of the land passed to the City of Yonkers as a city park. The rest was sold off.

So began a decline that lasted for over half a century. As this account reveals, however, it was not the end of the road for Untermyer's wondrous garden. Through decades when the property was buried under weeds and neglect, echoes of its former glory were glimpsed a few times by the well-meaning and the curious, and today, in its current state of restoration, the garden, in one form or another, has persisted.

As its chief advocate, Stephen Byrns, reflects, "The Untermyer Garden is awakening after seventy-five years of slumber." How pleased Samuel

Untermyer would have been to see such a thrilling recreation of his lost paradise on the Hudson.

Other gardens have been created by individuals whose personalities cannot be separated from their work. Vita Sackville-West's Sissinghurst and Frederick Law Olmsted's Central Park come to mind. Samuel Untermyer was an unlikely hero who put his heart and his fortune into creating a Shangri-La on the banks of the Hudson River. In these days of global uncertainty and environmental threat, the story of Untermyer's garden shines like a beacon of hope. It is his gift to the world, rescued and restored for generations to come.

The
CREATOR

"I'm told that my profession
is the law. But my real affection
is for my greenhouse."

—SAMUEL UNTERMYER, 1918

A Virginia-Born Lawyer
Takes New York

He was the "brilliant, slashing advocate, the tongue-stabber, the compeller of witnesses, the inexorable digger into secrets, the ardent, skillful wooer of public opinion." So wrote a journalist in 1907 of a man few people today have ever heard of. In the early years of the twentieth century, Samuel Untermyer made headlines almost every week, taking on the rich, the entrenched establishment, the robber barons, the most powerful corporations in America, the abusive husband, the greedy wife. With his "pitiless fire of questions," Untermyer put the fear of God into all those against whom he chose to make a case. He made millions with these skills, changing the face of American business. And yet he declared that "my real affection is for my greenhouse." Few people in New York in the 1900s would have believed that.

Samuel Untermyer was born in Lynchburg, Virginia, on March 2, 1858, the third of Therese and Isidor Untermyer's five children. Isidor owned a dry goods store, and for a while it did well, especially during the Civil War, when it provided uniforms for the Virginian soldiers. But the elder Untermyer seems not to have been a brilliant businessman, and among other mistakes, he invested in a disastrous tobacco manufacturing business. When he died in 1866, Isidor Untermyer was bankrupt. His middle son, Samuel, was 8 years old.

Therese, no doubt aware of her husband's flaws, had been conducting business on her own, investing in a boarding house and local real estate. Finding it impossible to make money in war-depressed Lynchburg,

A portrait of Untermyer as a young attorney, by Anders Zorn.

Therese moved her family to New York, where, shrewd as ever, she started a successful boarding house in an up-and-coming neighborhood on the Lower East Side of Manhattan, where many of her German-American friends from Virginia were resettling. Following the lead of a cousin and their half-brother, sons Isaac and Samuel went to New York law schools. At 18 years old, when Samuel started at Columbia Law School, he was already working as a clerk. When he graduated, he was only 20, too young

Short in stature, Untermyer was nonetheless
a formidable foe in the courtroom.

to appear in court. This did not deter the eager young lawyer. He grew a moustache and beard to disguise his youth and started his legal career underage, unrepentant, and unstoppable.

The first case that showed the New York legal world Samuel Untermyer was a lawyer to be reckoned with concerned his representation of a wealthy German-American brewer being sued for forgery. The prosecutors were a group of heavy hitters from New York's legal establishment. Samuel Untermyer, unassisted, won the case. He was 24 years old. The outcome was important enough to be reported in the *New York Times*, the first time the name Samuel Untermyer appeared in a newspaper—but certainly not the last. (The reporter spelled his name wrong, also not the last time.)

Samuel was very soon exploring more lucrative fields than simple litigation, such as the bond market in Britain. In so doing so, his firm became the only American law firm representing business interests in the United Kingdom. By 1897, Untermyer's aggressive moves were getting noticed. "Samuel Untermyer, who single-handed has been conducting a case involving $500,000 against 75 defendants," wrote a reporter for the *New York World*, "has gone to the front during the last 5 years faster than any man now practising at the New York bar, and the business done by his firm is enormous."

It's hard to imagine now, but in the last decade of the nineteenth century, Untermyer's was the only Jewish law firm on Wall Street. Until the arrival of the Jewish upstarts, the legal profession was almost entirely made up of white Anglo-Saxon Protestants, whose families had run the firms for generations. Not only were Samuel Untermyer and his partners extremely successful in general litigation, they also created new forms of legal instruments that the old-guard lawyers had never thought of—and that brought enormous new sources of wealth. The wall of class privilege crumbled with hardly a murmur.

The firm expanded rapidly. Two non-family members became partners: Samuel's brother-in-law Adolph Steinhardt, and perhaps more important, Louis Marshall, a German-American immigrant and friend of Samuel's since law school. Marshall had an unblemished record as a jurist and as a liberal Republican; he offered the firm useful contacts not already accessible. Also, as a passionate supporter of civil rights and Jewish causes, Marshall led Samuel into ways of thinking that were to deeply affect the younger man's future.

Guggenheimer, Untermyer & Marshall was quickly becoming the largest corporate law firm in the country. Untermyer had connections in every corner of the political and business world. Not bad for a German-American Jewish boy who had arrived in New York less than twenty years earlier.

An Unconventional Love Affair

Throughout his life, Samuel Untermyer considered himself a staunch Zionist, openly advocating for Jewish causes both in the United States and Europe. Yet in spite of this very public commitment, in 1880, at the age of 22, he met and fell in love with Minnie Carl, whose family were German Lutherans from St. Louis.

Minnie, at 23, was a year older than Samuel. She was the second of five children born to Manilius and Pauline Carl, both German immigrants. Manilius was a cultivated, elegant man who studied to be a violinist before going into the more lucrative newspaper business. He also brought scandal to the family, however, abandoning his wife and five children for the widow of a fellow Civil War soldier and moving to New York City. Pauline, a sturdy character, started a boarding house in St. Louis, but on hearing of her husband's comfortable life in New York, sold the business and brought her family to the city. Manilius and Pauline never divorced; Manilius later made some attempts to support his family, and was even a regular dinner guest.

Minnie, who was 9 years old when her father absconded, became a good seamstress and helped her mother by making clothes for her siblings. According to Untermyer family lore, she was a governess in the home of a Jewish client of Samuel Untermyer when she first met her future husband.

By the late 1880s, the young attorney had already built up a considerable reputation. Contemporary pictures of him show a young man with a leonine face, dark hair, piercing blue eyes, and a generous moustache. By the time he met Minnie, he was already developing an inimitable personal style, favoring tailored three-piece suits, starched collars, and elegant ties. His signature accessory was an orchid in his jacket lapel every day. For Minnie Carl, whose father had been a distant and unreliable presence, Samuel Untermyer's confident manner and skyrocketing career must have made a strong impression.

Though Minnie and Samuel were of different religions,
they shared German backgrounds and similar childhoods. By all accounts,
Minnie (seen here circa 1919) was the love of Samuel's life.

As for the young Untermyer, Minnie was the love of his life. She was of medium height, pretty, and passionately interested in the arts, particularly music, a love inherited from her father. Samuel shared Minnie's German background, and her intellectual sensibilities meshed brilliantly with his quick legal mind and European tastes. Both their mothers were single women in a man's world, and ran boarding houses to keep the families together. Samuel surely appreciated their similar experiences of difficult upbringings, and he recognized in Minnie a cultural sophistication that he lacked. She could give him entrée to an international circle of artists, writers, and musicians that had been denied him, a cultural leg up that would enhance his own standing as a man of the world.

The only obstacle to their future together was Samuel's mother Therese, who was horrified when her son told her he wished to marry a gentile. Untermyer dearly loved his mother, a strong woman who had shown exemplary devotion and courage in supporting the family during the challenging early years in New York. But was he now prepared to go against her deepest wishes? It seems that Samuel and Minnie's desire for each other was such that neither Therese nor conventional social mores were going to prevent the union. The couple proceeded to produce two children out of wedlock (one of whom did not survive). The family always remained silent on the matter, but it is remarkable that Samuel and Minnie were prepared to risk their reputations and perhaps his career on such eyebrow-raising behavior. With a baby, Alvin, already at home, Samuel married his Christian bride in October 1883.

The marriage was a success. Samuel and Minnie had three children in all: Alvin, who became a soldier, horseman, and lawyer; Irwin, who went on to become an appellate judge on the New York State Supreme Court; and Irene, a philanthropist. The family lived in a five-story townhouse on Fifth Avenue, with a cottage in Atlantic City, a rustic vacation home in upstate New York, and a seven-bedroom houseboat called the *Nirodha* in Florida. The couple also took regular vacations outside the country, often spending as many as three months abroad visiting Europe's cities and gardens. Serenity at home allowed Samuel Untermyer to focus his enormous energies without distraction on his career at the bar.

Scandals, Celebrities, and Chic Annulments

According to an admiring fellow New York attorney, Louis S. Levy, Untermyer was "savage and unrelenting in cross-examination, so keen and resourceful that nothing escaped or eluded him, he was a born prosecutor, brilliant, hard, and merciless. His withering sarcasm knew no restraint." This hard-charging technique was put to good use in an increasing number of much-publicized cases. Levy describes the lawyer's remarkable skills:

> As counsel to the Lockwood Committee [set up in 1919 to investigate rent and housing conditions in New York], he tore the heart out of iniquitous labor and building conditions in New York, bringing about many great reforms. To him, nothing was sacrosanct once he found an irregularity. In his work he was a veritable czar. Nothing could distract him once he started. In a committee investigation, Untermyer was supreme, if not omnipotent; as prosecutor, court, and jury, he tried the issues in his own fashion, he made the rulings conform to his wishes, and he wrote the verdict as he chose. The committee became merely a stage setting for him as the star performer.

Untermyer's ruthlessness was legendary. During the Lockwood hearings, he stopped a cross-examination and asked a witness to leave the stand. "What was wrong with him?" asked an associate. "One hundred percent honest," said Untermyer. In other words, Untermyer would not be able to get the witness to break in the way he wanted. As Levy said, "No lawyer was more astute as to what a given situation would yield, nor more effective in securing it." Untermyer's interrogations were frequently reported verbatim in the press. "The gentleman has punctuated my remarks again,"

Prominent New York attorney Samuel Untermyer (right) cuts a dapper figure with
John E. Laskey, U. S. Attorney for the District of Columbia, in the early 1900s.

one poor victim stammered in the witness box. "My intention was to
puncture rather than punctuate," responded Mr. Untermyer.

A historic case that added to the Untermyer legend was the Pujo scandal. In 1912, Untermyer was hired as lead counsel for an inquiry of the
Committee on Banking and Currency of the U. S. House of Representatives
into a so-called money trust, a secretive group of bankers and financiers
that had aroused a lot of rumors about corruption and other irregularities.

Named for the chairman of the committee, the Pujo hearings highlighted Untermyer's fearless dissection of several major banking titans, singling out J. P. Morgan, Paul Warburg, Jacob H. Schiff, and John D. Rockefeller. In this panoply of famous banking names, Morgan in particular was mercilessly interrogated by counsel for two grueling days. Three months later, the famous financier died, and his family wasted no time in accusing Untermyer of hastening the great man's death.

Untermyer's work on the Pujo committee led to the founding of the Federal Reserve System, an impressive outcome of his persistent struggle for fairness and transparency within the country's largest and most powerful institutions.

Another contemporary issue threatening the country's social fabric was the struggle for women's right to vote. Minnie Untermyer was a major supporter, joining committees and running bazaars to help the cause. But Samuel had beaten her to it. She admitted as much when she first gave her name to the cause in 1909, conceding that her husband "had always been a suffragist." So when the Men's League for Woman Suffrage was founded in 1910, the name Samuel Untermyer (identified as a "big gun" by the press) was right there along with other prominent male citizens. Untermyer also helped represent Margaret Sanger in the fight over birth control. In 1928, he led a debate against the death penalty that found less success than the women's suffrage movement, but it placed him publicly on the progressive side against his more conservative colleagues.

Much of this public crusading work was done for free, but Untermyer's financial ambitions were not so modest. At 21, he had already made over $75,000 dollars (over $4 million in today's currency). But that figure paled beside his later rewards; in 1910, his fee for the merger of the Boston Consolidated and the Utah Copper Companies (one of Untermyer's typically complex corporate briefs) was $775,000. Today that would be more than $18 million. The *New York Times* declared that it was the highest sum ever paid a lawyer in a single case. "Admiring lawyers gasp!" wrote the excited reporter.

UNTERMYER TO HELP

Will Advise Woman Suffragists on Legislative Work.

Samuel Untermyer is the newest member of the advisory committee on legislative work of the New York State Woman Suffrage Association. Others who will serve are George Foster Peabody, Mrs. James Laidlaw and Mrs. Roxana B. Burrows, who is chairman. It is intended to have a representative from every county on the committee, which will meet in Albany some time during the session. Miss Harriet May Mills, president of the association, said yesterday that the state would be organized by assembly districts as rapidly as possible. In this the association will co-operate with the Woman Suffrage party of New York City.

Samuel, always ahead of the times, became a vocal advocate
and supporter of women's suffrage.

Nor did Untermyer bestow his legal skills only on corporate or institutional clients. He took on anything that promised a lucrative outcome: criminal cases, personal disputes, conflicts that involved ordinary people across the country. Making emotional appeals to juries inspired his most dramatic performances; luminaries from the theater responded to this talent and clamored for his representation. Clients included New York theater titans the Shubert Brothers and David Belasco, opera star Geraldine Farrar, and Alexander Smith Cochran, a multimillionaire sportsman, in his divorce from Polish opera singer Ganna Walska.

In a two-part *New Yorker* profile published in 1930, Alva Johnston pointed to Untermyer's participation in "our most pretentious divorce cases and our most chic annulments." By this time Untermyer had become a celebrity, his clients the stuff of gossip. He even lent money to Adolph Ochs, owner of the *New York Times*, a gesture that surely did no harm to

Untermyer stepping out in New York City.

his coverage in that newspaper. "He surpasses all his contemporaries in the art of making the first page," said an observer.

Untermyer's client roster covered America's most prominent industries—businesses that had made their marks in motor vehicles, steel production, shipbuilding, gold mining, steam pumps, private banking, railways, and brewing, among others. If Untermyer was tough on big business, he was equally critical of his own profession. In an address to the New York Bar Association in 1909, he described his colleagues as "a lot of highly paid clerks to guide financiers in the way of keeping prayerfully in the law." He assailed the judges for incompetence, and the counselors for servility to the rich. Of course, the people in the street loved this populist rhetoric. Who until then had dared to abuse the stuffy legal profession so openly? Reporters flocked to his courtroom appearances, knowing they would get great copy.

Henry Ford, Anti-Semitism, and a Passionate Activist

Perhaps Samuel Untermyer's most influential contribution to the troubled world in which he lived was thanks to his political conscience. His partner Louis Marshall had already set the firm's policy by donating his time to civil rights groups such as the National Association for the Advancement of Colored People and the American Civil Liberties Union. In 1905, Marshall cofounded the American Jewish Committee, and worked tirelessly for the German-American-Jewish community and against anti-Semitism everywhere. Untermyer quickly took up the baton, and himself became involved in these causes, most notably in a vicious and long, drawn-out court battle against Henry Ford, the legendary automobile millionaire.

Ford was one of the richest and most popular businessmen in America, thanks to his company's invention of the Model T Ford. He started his anti-Semitic rants in 1915, but his lasting contribution (if that is what it can be called) to anti-Semitism in America was the publication of a series of anti-Jewish articles in the struggling weekly *Dearborn Independent*, which Ford bought for $1000 (about $18,000 today). By 1924, after hundreds of these inflammatory articles had appeared, the circulation had zoomed up to 700,000, almost as large as the largest daily newspaper in America, the *New York Daily News*. Capitalizing on this astonishing success, Ford and his team collected a selection of these pieces in a book called *The International Jew: The World's Foremost Problem*. This book was translated into sixteen languages and marked Ford as one of the most dangerous anti-Semites in the country. Since he was also considered by many

Untermyer's anti-Nazi appearances in the 1930s (here in New York City, at the microphone) were known to provoke violent hostility in the audience.

to be one of America's greatest heroes, the effect was devastating. Ford's name began to be linked with that of Adolf Hitler, and it was said Ford was offering financial support to the National Socialist Party in Berlin.

Jewish organizations sprang into action. Boycotts were organized against Ford products. Libraries banned the newspaper from their shelves. Sympathizers of the Jewish cause attempted to destroy all available copies of the book. A spate of lawsuits against Ford began to make their way through the courts, including a high-profile case brought by writer Herman Bernstein, one of the most litigious of Ford's enemies. Samuel Untermyer's senior partner, Louis Marshall, was Bernstein's lawyer.

Henry Ford, after numerous lawsuits that included one brought by Untermyer, issued a letter of apology pledging to suppress publication of an anti-Semitic book he had formerly produced.

The legal pressure on Ford finally began to take its toll, and in an astonishing pivot in 1927, Ford announced that he wished to make a formal apology and retract his anti-Semitic accusations. "I wish this wrong could be righted," he was quoted as saying.

To say this change of heart caused surprise is an understatement. Marshall was as surprised as everyone else, but of course he made the most of Ford's long and rambling mea culpa, which was extensively covered in the press. Ford said he wanted to "make amends" to his Jewish brothers, asking "their forgiveness for the harm I have intentionally committed." He even shut down the paper that had started it all, the *Dearborn Independent*.

Nobody familiar with Ford's years of ugly ravings believed a word of this, but Americans on the whole (many of whom had worshipped Ford), wanted to accept the apology and move on. Even many in the Jewish community embraced his change of heart. Louis Marshall warned against this naivete, and there were reservations elsewhere, but Ford had made a brilliant calculation. In a few years, his anti-Semitic history had been whitewashed almost out of existence. Almost, but not quite.

When Ford recanted, he signed a letter of apology to his most vocal adversary, Herman Bernstein, promising to suppress publication of the book. The two met at Greystone, Untermyer's country estate, in 1927, at which time Bernstein agreed to drop his suit. Untermyer, while accepting the conditions of the agreement, said the following:

> Wherever I went on my recent tour of the world, even into the most remote corners of the earth, in every county, city and hamlet, the Ford cars were to be found. Wherever there was a Ford car, there was a Ford agency not far away, and wherever there was a Ford agency these vile, libelous books in the language of that country were to be found. They, coupled with the name of Ford, have done more than could be undone in a century to sow, spread and ripen the poisonous seeds of anti-Semitism and race hatred . . . With that name, they spread like wildfire and became the bible of every anti-Semite . . .

Ford removed his name from the book, but it was not suppressed, and like Ford's prejudices, continued to work its evil. In his *New Yorker* profile of Untermyer, Alva Johnston said that some thought the lawyer's greatest achievement was making Henry Ford apologize to the Jews. But by the late 1930s, Ford was once more front and center in supporting Hitler's Nazi regime, and Untermyer knew that his work was not yet done.

There were other demands on Untermyer's time. While he never wavered from his Jewish loyalties, he was also an active Democrat, acting as delegate to the Democratic National Convention in 1904, 1908, and

1912, and delegate at large for the state of New York in 1916. His political ambitions were calculated enough, and he saw his chance when his friend Woodrow Wilson became president in 1912. The following year, Wilson signed the Federal Reserve Act, a radical shift in the country's banking system, and one which owed much to Untermyer's efforts. Wilson rewarded him for his many contributions to the party by appointing him in 1916 to serve on the United States section of the International High Commission, whose brief was to frame laws for the Pan-American countries. This was actually not quite what his friends had in mind—a cabinet post or ambassadorship was more in line with what they expected. Untermyer put a good face on it, however, declaring that he had only wished, interestingly, to become parks commissioner. It was said that Wilson decided against more prestigious advancement for his friend after some publicity arose over Untermyer's allegedly illegal stock profits (an accusation which was never proved) in a case dating back to the 1890s.

At the 1916 Democratic National Convention in St. Louis, Missouri, Untermyer served as a delegate at large.

World War I and Lost Pink Pajamas

With the outbreak of World War I in Europe in 1914, Samuel Untermyer had to grapple with far more complex issues than the possibility of cabinet posts. Because of his family roots and the notable list of German clients on his firm's roster, he initially threw his weight behind Germany. He was friendly with the German ambassador to the United States, giving him advice and in other ways assisting the German government in its propaganda push in America after the war had started. This soon became a toxic issue for Untermyer.

A story related by Minnie's grandson Frank Untermyer reveals how conflicted Untermyer felt at the time. In early 1916, when Sam and Minnie were in the presence of President Wilson, she tore off her diamonds, bracelets, and other jewelry, trying to persuade the president to stay out of the war. The scene embarrassed her husband enormously, but had no effect on Wilson.

It didn't help that Sam and Minnie were both vacationing in Carlsbad, Bavaria, when war broke out. In his usual flamboyant manner, Untermyer had booked the Prince's Suite at the Imperial Hotel, the most expensive hotel rooms in Europe. The breakout of war unfortunately wreaked havoc with his plans. He and Minnie had to be unceremoniously hustled to London and then crowded onto a ship back to New York with other rich American tourists, all forced to travel steerage. On docking in New York, he asserted to reporters that of their twelve trunks only two were lost (the press greatly enlarged these numbers), but he did admit that he yearned for "certain pink pajamas which can't be replaced." It's perhaps surprising that Untermyer, the sharpest of observers, failed so completely to realize that war was imminent.

After America entered the war in 1916, Untermyer's pro-German position became compromised, and he hastily withdrew his support from the country that was now his enemy. But the issue remained alive. Negative rumors were reported in the newspapers, and in 1918, Untermyer

Untermyer, left, and William Fox, founder of the Fox Film Corporation, at a Fox Film stockholders' meeting.

had to go before a Senate hearing in Washington to refute accusations of his pro-German activities. The press was relentless, and some never forgave him for his early support of Germany.

Untermyer received another blow in 1920 when Wilson, whom he had supported so loyally, lost the election. The Democrats found themselves out of office for twelve years, leaving Wilson's team chafing on the sidelines. But the ambitious Untermyer, now 62 years old, ignored the setback and with his characteristic energy, plunged into a series of high-profile cases, including the complex legal issues of the burgeoning film industry. Untermyer's theatrical connections served him well as he was called to represent the new powers in Hollywood such as Warner Brothers and Fox Film Corporation.

A signature Untermyer battle was over the New York subway system. He became pro bono counsel for the New York City Transit Commission in 1926, in a series of long, drawn-out suits about rules, regulations, and fares that lasted several years. In 1931, Untermyer dramatically resigned, declaring that the case, which he was losing, was not in the interests of the people of the city. While he failed to unify the subway system, he managed to retain the five-cent fare, a victory for the people of New York that became one of Untermyer's most impressive achievements—and made him a hero to all the strap-hangers in the city.

His international reputation also skyrocketed after he was appointed negotiator for the surrender of several royal estates in Austria after its defeat in World War I. The dismemberment of large chunks of the Austrian Empire was witnessed with enthusiasm by the victorious Allies, eager to benefit from these complex transactions. The fact that Samuel Untermyer was largely responsible for the deal hashed out at the Ritz Hotel in Paris in 1921 showed once more his legendary powers of persuasion—a talent neither the Europeans nor the Americans would soon forget.

Love, Death, and the Garden

In 1899, at the peak of his financial success, Untermyer bought Greystone, a 99-room, turreted mansion along with a 113-acre estate on the Hudson River. It had belonged to the retired governor of New York, Samuel J. Tilden.

The custom had been well established in feudal England and France for the royal favorites of the day to accumulate an extensive amount of real estate, and the more splendid and sumptuous the mansions and gardens, the more eminence attached to the illustrious figures who owned them. The newly minted titans of industry and finance in nineteenth-century America were happy to adopt this tradition, spending their vast fortunes on palaces and parks that mimicked the great estates of Europe, importing rooms from Paris, art from Rome, and parterres from Hampton Court to

Greystone, the mansion in Yonkers that belonged to New York
Governor Samuel Tilden, circa 1886.

dazzle the local peasantry. Not surprisingly, Untermyer was eager to take part in the building boom engaged in by his peers. Being Untermyer, of course, he would do it better.

Greystone cost him $171,500, not a huge strain on his prodigious bank account. The house itself had few of the aesthetic graces his Europe-loving peers favored. In fact, Untermyer did not make a point generally of spending his money on architecture and interior decoration.

While many millionaires of the time entered with gusto into the international art market, decorating the walls of their mansions with great paintings, Untermyer was more restrained. He attended auctions and bought from several dealers, though few of the purchases made headlines. Acquisitions included a Cellini bronze, a Rodin head, many large tapestries, a group of Indian miniatures. He supported American artists—Winslow Homer, Homer Martin, George Inness—who were not very

Greystone, after its purchase by Samuel Untermyer in 1899.

fashionable at the time. At the height of his collecting period, he owned a Whistler, a Rubens, a Gainsborough, a Sir Thomas Lawrence, a Van Dyck, a Joshua Reynolds, two Monets, and two Corots. Impressive today, but only the Whistler and the Rubens seemed notable to connoisseurs of the time.

It soon became obvious to everyone that however its new owner felt about Greystone, it was the house's strikingly attractive surrounding real estate, developed by the previous owner, Samuel Tilden, that Untermyer had his eye on. Shortly after his purchase, Untermyer went on an acquisition spree, extending the estate to 150 acres along the banks of the river. In 1916, he summoned William Welles Bosworth, the famous Beaux-Arts

An 1870 watercolor by John William Hill shows the idyllic view of the Palisades from a Yonkers estate not far from Greystone, with the sloping land marked by rocky outcroppings.

architect who had spent many years working at Kykuit, the Rockefellers' grand estate in Pocantico Hills, to his site. Untermyer instructed Bosworth to make him "the finest garden in the world."

It wasn't as though Untermyer was ignorant of gardens. His chief horticulturist later said that his employer knew as much about plants as he did. Untermyer said his love of flowers came from his mother, when he was growing up in Virginia. "From the time I could understand anything, I have regarded flowers as an inseparable part of daily life," he declared. Perhaps it is not surprising, then, that after all his years in the city making his fortune, he should, at the pinnacle of his career, turn to a passion that had simmered within him since childhood. Untermyer was 41 when he bought Greystone. He had achieved great fame and made millions in the practice of law. It was time for him to turn his enormous

Based on what William Welles Bosworth had designed
for Kykuit, the Rockefeller estate, Untermyer hired Bosworth
to create a grand garden at Greystone.

reserves of energy and money toward a quite different venture: a dream
of paradise on earth.

Hiring Bosworth was typical Untermyer—ready to do almost anything
to challenge his rivals. He was so competitive that at one point he bred
collie dogs at Greystone for the sole purpose of besting J. P. Morgan's
famous dog-show winners. Now he was determined to take on John D.
Rockefeller in the garden stakes. Untermyer greatly respected Rockefeller's mind, and Kykuit was the talk of New York. How better to claim
victory than by acquiring Rockefeller's lead architect?

The high, crenellated walls and gate of the Walled Garden in its heyday,
scored with a diamond pattern.

Until his death in 1940, Untermyer continued to refine and expand
a fantasy landscape that became a legend. Throughout the 1920s, while
taking on some of the largest and most complex cases ever heard before
the courts, he would mull over plants and plant materials with his gardeners. He attacked witnesses in the dock just as energetically as ever, but

Today, colorful leaves set off the wall and a corner tower of the Walled Garden in autumn.

also applied himself to the design of new flower gardens, cultivating rare species of orchids and experimenting with exotic fruits and vegetables.

It is said that Louis XIV's penchant for leading large tours of foreigners through his spectacular gardens at Versailles, unusual for a reigning monarch, was not simply to impress, but to intimidate. Samuel Untermyer had something of the French king's swagger. He was happy to overwhelm his opponents at the bar. But he saw his gardens differently. He wanted them to be enjoyed by others as much as he enjoyed them himself. To this end, he insisted that the gardens be open to the public every Tuesday, an example of the democratic spirit that his rivals up in Pocantico Hills or Newport were not quick to imitate.

An early view of the walls, canals, and circular temple at Greystone.

Minnie Untermyer was a willing collaborator in her husband's extravagant undertaking. Sometimes she might go to an auction and buy something for the house on his behalf—not always with his approval. (She once bought several Stanford White ceilings that remained in storage until Samuel's death.) She shared her husband's interest in horticulture, and was credited with the cultivation of the Untermyer rhododendrons, which won first prize at the flower show of the American Horticultural Society in 1910 and for years after. But Minnie's greatest influence may have been in the architectural layout of the garden, for part of her husband's dream was to provide her with the perfect setting for her artistic and social ventures.

By the early 1920s, the Untermyers' gardens had become renowned not only for their horticultural and architectural beauty but also for the

Very different flowers, shrubs, and trees complement the temple today.

entertainment presented there. Untermyer had turned Yonkers into a kind of Hollywood. It was said that when the new owner of Greystone started commuting to New York from Greystone in his bright yellow carriage, a neighbor complained that he violated the local speed limit, and a patrolman was assigned to keep an eye on him. His reputation at the wheel was such that at 8:30 every morning, children lined the curb to see him leave. For some of the locals at least, this dashing, flower-obsessed lawyer was a colorful addition to the neighborhood.

But the Untermyers' happiness was cruelly cut short. In 1923, when Minnie was traveling in Europe, she was stricken with appendicitis. "She was operated on there by a celebrated surgeon," said the *New York Times* obituary, "and recovered before she returned to America. Last autumn, however, she suffered an attack of paralysis while attending a performance at the Metropolitan Opera House. The attack rendered her practically an invalid up to the time of her death." Samuel and their three children were at her bedside when she died. Her distraught husband bought for her a 22,000-square-foot plot in Woodlawn Cemetery in the Bronx—second in size only to Jay Gould's. Samuel spared no expense on this garden of remembrance. Paul Chalfin, the artistic supervisor of Villa Vizcaya, a glamorous estate in Miami, designed the mausoleum, and Gertrude Vanderbilt Whitney, just beginning to make her name as a sculptor, created the bronze monument that adorns it.

Samuel and Minnie had been a brilliant couple. Samuel loved Minnie's family as his own. Their mothers had had very similar experiences as single women struggling with large families in New York, and both admirable women died the same year. They shared the same political views, most notably when Samuel took the lead in the women's suffrage movement. With her bitter experience of a wayward father, Minnie probably whispered a thing or two in Samuel's ear during his more sensational divorce cases. Occasionally he would write testy letters to her, scolding her for buying furniture or decorating fixtures at exorbitant prices: "I would like to know what on earth the enclosed bill means." Like most self-made millionaires, he hated the idea of being taken advantage of, and Minnie occasionally went overboard in the auction rooms. But their joint interests in the arts and the gardens at Greystone remained strong until the end.

Some said Samuel Untermyer never got over the death of his wife. His grief was evident for all to see. He tried to deal with his loss in the only way he knew how—by rushing into action. He quickly decided to embark on a four-month trip to the Far East on the Red Star Line. He booked the largest suite on the ship, taking out all the suite's furniture and replacing it with his own from Greystone, including bed, chairs, lamps, and rugs. But this distraction did not keep him away from his work for long. He had worked nonstop for forty years, and couldn't stop, although the repercussions soon became apparent. His asthma, from which he had

Gertrude Vanderbilt Whitney was asked to create a bronze sculpture for the Untermyer Memorial in Woodlawn Cemetery when Minnie died.

suffered since childhood, grew steadily worse. His habit of getting only a few hours of sleep a night, which had been the subject of admiring articles in the local press, became less tolerable for him.

Friends also observed a change in his professional life. After two decades of bruising confrontations in the courtroom, he began to be almost mellow on the stand, to take on more pro bono work, and to accept cases that did not involve millions of dollars. In one lawsuit, he defended a young, working-class woman who confessed to murdering her husband. With this handicap, Untermyer played so brilliantly on the jury's sympathies—explaining that the woman was simply defending herself—that she was acquitted. Untermyer was awarded $500 for his efforts, which he immediately gave to his grateful client. "I have made enough money," he once said. "More would only bother me. Now I am going to help my fellow men."

Einstein, Hitler, and a New Rival

At the beginning of the 1930s, Untermyer was summoned back into the thick of the action, entering into perhaps the most public and controversial phase in his career—as a crusader against Nazism.

Untermyer's commitment was already unassailable, thanks to the wrenching legal confrontations with Henry Ford, which alerted him and so many others to the evil elements of fascism. But he found a kindred spirit in a new client, perhaps the most significant client he acquired after the First World War. This was not an international corporate or business tycoon, but a German physicist named Albert Einstein.

Untermyer met Einstein in 1921 on one of the lawyer's frequent visits to Europe. That year, Einstein was awarded the Nobel Prize in Physics. Untermyer was not a scientist, but he and Einstein got on well together. Einstein, like Untermyer, was a passionate Zionist and supporter of civil rights, but he also shrewdly estimated that "the most famous lawyer in New York," as he called Untermyer, might help him in more personal matters. Einstein's fees and expenses were becoming increasingly complicated, thanks to the success of the Nobel winner's public lectures, books, and articles, both at home and abroad. Einstein was also worried about the darkening political situation in Germany. Happy to help his friend, Untermyer transferred some of Einstein's money out of Germany to the United States, for safekeeping and investment. Since there were severe restrictions and tax liabilities in Germany at that time on the export of foreign currency, the activities of various American banks on Einstein's behalf were communicated to him in code. Untermyer's hand in all this was unmistakable.

Albert Einstein became first a client, then a friend of Samuel Untermyer's in the early 1930s, when the Nazi presence in Germany was first gaining a foothold.

Several of Einstein's academic friends were eager to share in this obviously fruitful American connection, but Einstein was rather cagey about lending out his lawyer. Einstein's only advice to them was that "self-assured forthrightness is necessary anywhere in America, otherwise you don't get anything paid for and are looked down on."

By the early 1930s, it was clear to Untermyer and Einstein that what was happening in Germany was a danger not only to world peace, but to humanity itself. Untermyer began making speeches across the country, warning of Hitler's plans and the catastrophe to come. As founder and president of the Non-Sectarian Anti-Nazi League, he tried to defuse the increasing pressure of Nazi propaganda, and helped organize a boycott of all German goods. In August of 1933, he gave a remarkably prescient speech on WABC radio that was published in its entirety in the *New York Times*. In it, he proclaimed the following:

> We owe it not only to our persecuted brethren but to the entire world to now strike in self-defense a blow that will free humanity from a repetition of this incredible outrage. This time the Jews are the victims, next time it may be the Catholics or Protestants. If we once admit, as is brazenly insisted by the German Government, that such fiendish persecution of the people of one race or creed is an internal domestic affair and not a world concern, how are we to know whose turn will be next?

During his trip to Europe, friends had asked him to meet Hitler. "I have no intention of going to see Hitler," he replied. "It is an essential part of the Hitler policy that the Jew shall be persecuted to the point of extermination." One can only wonder that as early as 1933, Samuel Untermyer read the tea leaves so accurately.

At this point, any lingering loyalties to Untermyer's German roots had vanished. Indeed, the German government was infuriated by his much-publicized hostility and encouraged attacks against him. At a large convention of American Nazis at Madison Square Garden in 1934, chants of "Hang him, hang him!" greeted him when he appeared on the podium. He was not deterred. He kept up a relentless barrage of speeches and articles against the Third Reich. He was photographed at mass meetings, giving impassioned addresses to the large crowds who came to hear him. He called on Jews and non-Jews alike to make common cause against Hitler, challenging that "the slaughter, starvation, and annihilation of its own innocent and defenseless citizens" was not, as German leadership asserted, an "internal affair."

He continued to drum up support for an economic boycott that would undermine the Hitler regime. "How can these gentlemen, most of whom, strange to say, are themselves Jews, refuse the most active, aggressive

Untermyer actively spoke out in opposition at pro-Nazi conventions held in America.
This one at Madison Square Garden in 1934 attracted 20,000 attendees.

cooperation to this struggle of civilization against medieval savagery?" he demanded. But it was not a popular idea, even in the Jewish community, and most businesses did not cooperate, although department stores such as Gimbels, Sears, and Woolworth gave in to his pressure. Again and again, Untermyer urged Americans to "drive the last nail in the coffin of bigotry and fanaticism that has dared raise its ugly head to slander, belie and disgrace twentieth-century civilization." It's no wonder that the British press called him "Hitler's bitterest foe." He himself confirmed it, saying, "I am told that I have the distinction of being the most thoroughly hated and reviled man in Germany," adding, with a typical Untermyer flourish, "I am proud of that distinction and hope only that it is well earned."

His commitment occasionally led to violence. On a cruise back from Bermuda in late 1934, Untermyer got into an argument with his fellow passengers when he insisted they throw overboard all the carnival and Christmas decorations on the ship marked "made in Germany." The fight became physical, and he took the blows in stride. But the endless rallies and confrontations wore him down, and his health again began to betray him. Inspired by visits to California, in 1929, he bought a small villa in Palm Springs called The Willows, where he felt the warm, dry climate would help his failing heart and lungs. As his health wavered, he began spending more time there.

It is easy to see why he fell in love with The Willows. The Italian-style cottage seemed to emerge from a series of dramatic granite boulders, down which poured a waterfall that acted as a backdrop to the elegant dining patio outside the living room. Beneath the garden, an ancient stream called the Tahquitz Ditch, lined with willows, gurgled through a rock-lined pathway and pooled in a shady glade. Behind the house, a trail led up the rocky hillside, offering spectacular views of the Palm Springs desert. Best of all, the previous owners had been keen gardeners and had planted the hillsides with banana, peach, and orange trees; coffee plants; bushes of brightly colored bougainvillea; and other tropical trees and shrubs. How serene the intimate atmosphere of this flower-filled place must have felt to Untermyer after the vast, haunted rooms of Greystone. The rocks and waterfall at The Willows would have been a pleasing reminder—in miniature—of his rock garden in Yonkers. For a man who had spent most of his career in the most grandiose enclaves of power and wealth, to choose this simple, welcoming villa as his second home confirms that the litigious lawyer had not lost his soul.

During the remainder of the 1930s, Untermyer spent extended time at The Willows, where he felt his strength slowly returning. He made few changes in the landscape, except to add palm trees and a collection of orchids, always his favorite flower. Naturally enough, after a lifetime of

Untermyer (far right) often entertained at The Willows,
here hosting (left to right) Albert Einstein, Mrs. Warren Pinney,
German film director Ernst Lubitsch, and Einstein's wife, Elsa.

community and social awareness, he couldn't resist weighing in on local issues, warning against the spread of trailer parks and suggesting the new location of the airport, for instance. But his primary activity during these final years was entertaining. Friends from all over the world, celebrities, politicians, and intellectuals, came to visit. Shaking off the lonely years after Minnie's death, he was once again a vital and amusing host, often in the company of a young friend, Molly McAdoo, the stepdaughter of an old friend from the Wilson years, Bill McAdoo. Untermyer had represented Molly in two divorces, and she now found a regular place at The Willows as his hostess and companion.

So these years in California, in spite of Untermyer's failing health, were full of life and interest. However ill he was, he never lowered his standards when welcoming the many distinguished guests who showed up on his doorstep. Visitors included luminaries ranging from New York's colorful mayor, Jimmy Walker, to newspaper magnate William Randolph Hearst; from author Upton Sinclair to *New York Times* publisher Adolph S. Ochs. A photograph from the time shows the host in a wicker lounge chair, sporting his signature three-piece suit, cravat, and in his lapel, an orchid—airmailed fresh once a week. This was the Samuel Untermyer of legend, and he never let anyone forget it.

His friend Albert Einstein was also a frequent visitor. Einstein loved The Willows and its beautiful setting. In 1931, the physicist wrote, "Wonderful sunrise from outlook above the Untermayer [sic] villa. Sun comes up on the desert mountains and goldens the former plumb-grey rocks behind our viewpoint." In a later letter, after describing another enjoyable evening with his host, Einstein added the rather sad comment, "He became very pessimistic over the years."

The Untermyer Gardens in Yonkers retained their magic, even if the maestro was not at home. But the times were not favorable to these frivolous pleasures. The pessimism Einstein had sensed in Untermyer had cause. Even as attendance records were being broken at the Untermyer

When Untermyer was at The Willows in Palm Springs,
his lapel orchids were airmailed fresh once a week.

Gardens, halfway around the world, Hitler was sowing seeds of a very different kind, seeds that would grow into an epidemic that could not be contained. Even Samuel Untermyer, described as one of the greatest advocates who ever lived, could not prevent the genocide that was to come. "He foresaw the terrible cataclysm which was imminent, and he contributed all his power and resources to avert and to combat it," his friend Louis Levy wrote.

But Untermyer was old and tired and increasingly unwell. His last visit to Greystone may have been in October 1939, when he was seen mingling with the record crowds of that day, accompanied by his son, Irwin. The sight of so many visitors must have cheered him greatly. Five months later, on March 16, 1940, back at The Willows, with his son Alvin at his side, Samuel Untermyer died at the age of 82. Perhaps he was fortunate to go at that moment. He escaped bearing witness to the devastation of the Second World War, which he had so accurately predicted and worked so desperately to prevent.

The obituaries were uniformly lavish in their praise. "One of the great lawyers and masterful public figures of the last fifty years," wrote the *New York Herald Tribune*. "He was one of the leading lawyers of our time and a man of unusual forcefulness and of indomitable courage," said Governor Herbert H. Lehman. "He was fair and broad-minded," observed Mayor Fiorello H. LaGuardia, continuing, "On many occasions he had the courage to differ with his associates when it was unpopular to do so." U. S. Senator Robert F. Wagner summed him up with palpable sadness, noting, "As a leader of the bar, patron of the arts and of innumerable charitable endeavors, champion of public causes and defender of the rights of man in every land, he won the admiration and deep affection of his countrymen in every phase and walk of life."

Samuel Untermyer's body was brought from Palm Springs to New York for burial. George H. Chisholm, Untermyer's estate manager at Greystone, decorated his master's funeral casket with 300 orchids and 10,000 lilies of the valley, all plucked from the conservatories at Greystone. Samuel was laid to rest at Woodlawn Cemetery, next to his beloved Minnie. One hundred fifty of the famous Untermyer rhododendrons were planted in the great man's memory.

The
ARCHITECTURE

"A creation both highly individual
and beautiful."

—WILLIAM WELLES BOSWORTH, 1918

William Welles Bosworth and the Beaux-Arts Tradition

When Samuel Untermyer bought the late Governor Tilden's castle-like mansion on the Hudson River, his first order of business was to improve its rather forbidding appearance. As a visitor said about the mansion, there was "a general feeling of heaviness and want of light." Untermyer hired architect J. H. Freedlander to open up the place with bay windows, new staircases, and stained glass in the ceilings. The interiors were refurbished and new plumbing installed. The only place where Untermyer lavished serious resources was in his sleeping quarters. There, in a large white tile room, he installed a luxurious plunge bath of massive width and depth, in which a person could be completely immersed. "This swimming tank is lined with white marble and the water which bubbles from the mouths of silver fish can be kept at any desired temperature," wrote an awed reporter.

A large limestone porch was added, approached by a new carriage road, and various improvements were made to the existing outbuildings, all at a cost of around $100,000. Governor Tilden had made some landscaping efforts close to the house on the lines of what a gentleman farmer might enjoy. Untermyer's vision was far grander. He was going to create a garden that would compete with the greatest gardens in Europe, if not the world.

For this extravagant dream he needed more land. Over time, he purchased an ornate Victorian pile nearby called Duncraggan, owned by Eva Smith Cochran, a rich philanthropic widow whose father had been one of the manufacturing millionaires in Yonkers. Untermyer also added to his expanding acreage with a property belonging to William B. Smith, whose family, like the Cochrans, made their fortune in carpets. Some of

Garden designer Ellen Biddle Shipman was hired in 1925 to restore Henry Wadsworth Longfellow's garden, shown here. But the majority of landscape design at the time was done by (mostly male) architects.

the Untermyer children occasionally lived at Duncraggan, but they complained it was full of mice and rats. Both properties were later demolished. It was on this extensive stretch of land on the banks of the Hudson River that William Welles Bosworth was to make his mark.

In the United States, landscape architecture at the turn of the nineteenth century was a fledgling offspring of the building arts. While a few—mostly women, including Ellen Biddle Shipman and Edith Wharton's niece, Beatrix Farrand—were making a name for themselves in garden design, most landscape designers were architects who did a bit of garden design on the side. The new millionaires who were building their mansions and palaces wanted large, sweeping landscapes like the ones they saw on their European travels. The gardens of Versailles were on their minds when they hired architects to produce their extravaganzas back home.

Responding to this need, most American architects at this time felt it de rigueur to acquire their architectural training in Europe, specifically at the École des Beaux-Arts in Paris. It was a grueling course, focusing exclusively on the classical arts of ancient Greece and Rome, which the students had to study and then translate into their own works. One commentator characterized it as "putting up little Romes everywhere." Almost all the big names in American architecture in the late nineteenth century, including Thomas Hastings, Richard Morris Hunt, Charles McKim, H. H. Richardson, Louis Sullivan, and Marion Sims Wyeth were graduates of this school. Many public buildings we admire today show the influence of these architects' Paris training, such as the public libraries of New York and Boston and New York's Grand Central Station.

The apotheosis of the Beaux-Arts influence occurred at the World's Columbian Exposition in Chicago in 1893, where in a remarkable homage to the principles of the École, almost every major building in the exposition was designed in the neoclassical style. While some delighted in this "triumph of classicism and of a nation," others were appalled by such a slavish devotion to antiquated, borrowed styles, the so-called architecture of antiquity. Sullivan commented that the Chicago Fair set back American architecture fifty years.

William Welles Bosworth was an exemplar of the École des Beaux-Arts. His career before he met Samuel Untermyer was firmly rooted in neoclassicism, with experience gained in London with Sir Lawrence Alma-Tadema, a proponent of classical forms and ornaments, and with two American architectural firms solidly identified with the classical style—Shepley, Rutan and Coolidge, and Carrère and Hastings. In 1907, Bosworth won the major commission of his life, to work on Kykuit, in the Pocantico Hills, the vast estate of John D. Rockefeller. He worked there, off and on, for over twenty years.

Whether Samuel Untermyer knew or cared about the controversy over American neoclassicism is not recorded. What is known is that he knew about Kykuit, and visited it at least once, in so doing acquiring

École des Beaux-Arts.

Most American architects of the time trained at the École des Beaux-Arts in Paris.

a small stone fountain which apparently didn't go well in the Rockefeller gardens and found a home at Greystone. What is better known is that Untermyer was competitive to his bones, and if Rockefeller's Kykuit was the spectacular place everyone said it was, then it was up to Untermyer to go one better at Greystone. And what better way to achieve this goal than by spiriting away the man most responsible for Kykuit's success—William Welles Bosworth. At their meeting, according to Bosworth, Untermyer asked him to design "the finest garden in the world."

By 1911, Bosworth seems to have become somewhat conflicted about the Beaux-Arts training he and many of his colleagues had absorbed so thoroughly. In an article he wrote in *The American Architect* about his work at Kykuit, he seemed to disparage the overwhelming influence of the Roman columns, fountains, and arches that popped up in so many American gardens. "No home was complete without a pergola," he complained. (Frank Lloyd Wright, for one, called these ornate furnishings "Frenchite pastry.") Bosworth also grumbled about dealers importing "all sorts of so-called garden ornaments, presumably antique. Fountains and troughs are found mixed in with classic and English and French vases, benches and sundials . . . " He concluded that the "resulting incoherence is [due to the fact that] lacking a tradition at home, our minds are furnished with pictures of every sort of foreign garden." Bosworth bemoaned the fact that the lack of tradition at home inevitably meant that American gardens "have no pure historic style."

Bosworth's work at the Rockefeller estate Kykuit, shown here, likely influenced Untermyer's selection of Bosworth for the design of Greystone's gardens.

The orangerie at Kykuit, in Pocantico Hills, New York, where Bosworth honed his skills as an architect for the Rockefeller family.

From Kykuit to Greystone

Bosworth summarized his own theory of landscape architecture quite simply and sensibly. He proposed that owners whose land lay over lowland valleys might find beauty more easily attained by studying the English method of perfecting groups of trees, glimpses of water, and winding paths. On the other hand, he said, "For the proprietor whose house stands on a hill with the ground falling steeply away toward the view, he will surely achieve more beauty by studying the terrace treatment so preferred by the Italians." He also repeated the well-known principle that the house determined the disposition of the garden, and that "ideally they should be built together."

The Italianate Tea House at Kykuit, designed by Bosworth.

The Kykuit estate, when Bosworth first saw it, was impressive enough, at least 2000 acres rising 500 feet above the Hudson River. "On a clear day one can easily see the Singer Building Tower," he wrote admiringly. "The place is so extensive that one may drive some twenty miles without leaving it." John D. Rockefeller Jr. had bought the land for his aging father, and had originally chosen the New York architecture firm of Delano and Aldrich to build the house in the neoclassical Beaux-Arts style. However, after its completion in 1908, Rockefeller didn't like the front façade and it was largely rebuilt, along with an extended forecourt and other additions, by Bosworth himself, who forged at this time a close friendship with his client's son. These changes, with contributions from the young Rockefeller, were mostly completed in 1915—good timing, as this was just as Untermyer was preparing to employ Bosworth himself.

It remains for the Kykuit visitor to decide if Bosworth avoided the "incoherence" he criticized elsewhere in American landscape designs. Bosworth was familiar with Edith Wharton's much-admired book, *Italian Villas and Their Gardens*, published in 1904, and her descriptions of the layouts and ornamentation of classical Italian gardens gave him several ideas for Kykuit. Yet while Rockefeller's gardens are firmly in the tradition of neoclassicism, there's no question that they are influenced by other cultures. There are Japanese gardens, boxwood and English ivy, spring bulb gardens, topiary, and many water features with canals, fountains, and jets of water in the Moorish style.

Bosworth's first exposure to Untermyer's location in Yonkers was very different. Unlike the mostly undeveloped landscape surrounding Kykuit, Yonkers by this time had become a small but booming hilltown community, with successful manufacturing businesses and an active waterfront, furnishing goods to New York City. In 1894, the *New York*

Loved in Europe, boxwood was a choice by Bosworth for both Kykuit and Greystone—a selection that Untermyer endorsed.

Yonkers was becoming a booming community in the early 1900s,
even hosting its own marathon.

Times praised Yonkers as a "beautiful suburb of the great metropolis."
The article pointed out that one could get home to Yonkers from midtown
Manhattan in thirty minutes by motor car—surely an attraction for the
workaholic Untermyer. "The social aspects of the city," said the reporter,
"cannot be too highly spoken of, embracing intelligence and culture and
wealth." In short, Yonkers was considered one of the most prosperous
and desirable localities in Westchester County. It also encompassed large
expanses of land along the river, where people took walks and picnicked
on summer days and enjoyed some of the most spectacular views found
anywhere on the Eastern seaboard. It was alongside this community that
Untermyer's estate resided: 150 acres, mostly forming a long stretch of
land alongside the river, with the dramatic cliffs of the Palisades rearing
up from the opposite banks.

Yonkers City Hall, circa 1933.

But a close study of this property must have given Bosworth pause. The Kykuit estate was far larger than Untermyer's; he would have much less to work with. Also, the crenellated mansion, Greystone, was not nearly as well sited as Kykuit, which had a higher elevation and therefore a better view. Furthermore, as Bosworth himself noted, ideally the house and garden should be conceived in the same breath, designed at the same time, and able to relate to each other in architectural terms, as had been satisfyingly rendered at Kykuit. In Untermyer's case, the house had been built earlier than the garden now being planned, thus making it impossible to combine the styles of house and garden. Greystone stood on its own, without the usual European-style view over parterres or forecourts that would be available to a visitor looking out of a window or standing on a balcony. Versailles it was not—and could never be.

The rough, irregular parts of Greystone's landscape presented a challenge for Bosworth in planning the gardens.

To make the task more challenging, Greystone was surrounded by uneven, rocky terrain, seriously unfriendly to the idea of the formal garden required by traditional Beaux-Arts rules. Indeed, unlike Kykuit's lawn-like slopes, most of Untermyer's land was wildly irregular, with many stone outcroppings, hillocks, mounds, and dips, often steeply graded down to the Hudson. Random clumps of trees and large boulders jutted out of the ground in various places. Kykuit was a billiard table by comparison. How was Bosworth to create a properly formal landscape in such terrain—let alone come up with a plan dissimilar enough, and fabulous enough, to eclipse, at least in Untermyer's eyes, all the work he had done for Rockefeller?

The New Client's Challenge

In December 1918, Bosworth published an article in *The Architectural Review* describing the complexities of his commission. (This was also the year he wrote to the American Institute of Architects requesting that "William" be removed from his name.) He wrote:

> The present owner of the estate, whose extensive greenhouses testify to his fondness for growing things, wanted a scheme to provide space for the cultivation of all kinds of flowers, fruits, and shrubs, with proper adjusts in trees, water, and architectural effects. But the only place for a garden of this type was the site of a previous garden, i.e. to the north of the existing greenhouses, and at some distance from the house. The contour of the ground seemed to lend itself to a system of two terraces, one a few feet below the other, and as the east boundary of the site is quite near an important artery of travel, a high wall, to give the garden privacy and to cut it off from the noise of automobiles, seemed an essential point of departure in the determination of the architectural treatment.

Already the differences between the Untermyer and Rockefeller agendas were becoming apparent. Rockefeller wanted a spring and fall garden because the family did not live at Kykuit during the summer. Bosworth designed Kykuit "with the one thought of its owner's pleasure in providing a variety of walks and places to sit and enjoy views." Untermyer's emphasis from the outset was on the cultivation of plants. Horticulture was his passion. The walks and places to sit were secondary.

What Bosworth privately felt about this, he did not say. But he certainly had to think outside the parterre box in order to work with this erratically uneven, sometimes rocky, landmass. He had to somehow come up with a unifying form for the whole landscape, with its undulating contours and existing buildings, including the two smaller houses and

An early photo of the canal leading to the amphitheater, in the Walled Garden.

The corners of the Walled Garden are punctuated by octagonal towers
such as those seen in Persian and Mughal palaces, one of
the reasons Bosworth referred to the garden as "Indo-Persian."

the greenhouses. The greenhouses in particular were bones of contention. Installed by previous owner Tilden and not appreciated by Bosworth, they were central to Untermyer's plans for plant cultivation.

Bosworth had to come up with a dramatic idea to give shape and form to the rest of the landscape that would satisfy his demanding client and also fulfill his own ambitions. His solution was to embrace the greenhouses as a kind of elongated portal to a formal landscape that included six main sections: the Walled Garden, the Vista, the Color Gardens, the Rose Garden, the Vegetable Gardens, and, finally, high up on a rocky promontory, the Temple of Love.

The most important architectural construction was the Walled Garden, although it was not always called that. In the short and only essay he published about designing Untermyer's garden, Bosworth said that

Walls of the Walled Garden were tall enough to hide the greenhouses.

the special conditions of the land inspired him to create what he called an "Indo-Persian type of garden." Many of these so-called Mughal gardens, he explained, were rectangular in form, with a cross of waterways intersecting at the center and bordered by flower beds. "They had kiosks and porticoes between the levels or around the boundaries of the gardens, and were nearly always surrounded by high walls." In other words, Bosworth decided, in a complete departure from European models, to create a roughly three-acre, three-walled Persian garden, with walls high enough to conceal the greenhouses. The side without a wall was left open to reveal vistas of the river and the Palisades beyond.

The garden contained some Grecian aspects, however, and with Greek design a popular theme of the era, Untermyer began calling it the Greek Garden, as did the press. The garden's three enclosed sides were created

Diamond-shaped scores were repeated in the walls and in other areas of the Walled Garden

by high, crenellated walls made of creamy beige brick, inset with decorative panels in cream-colored stucco. These were scored with a diamond pattern. A visitor familiar with Mughal architecture might, at first viewing of these patterned walls, be reminded of the Agra Fort in northern India. At each of the four corners of the garden were octagonal towers such as those seen in Persian and Mughal palaces (called *chatri* in India). Bosworth once told Rockefeller that he admired a book called *Gardens of the Great Mughals*, published in 1913 by C. M. Villiers Stuart, which showed many photographs of the canals, basins, pavilions, and terraces that Bosworth studied so carefully and adapted for Greystone.

Originally this garden could only be reached by walking past the Tilden greenhouses, which blocked the view from the house and diminished the impact of the garden walls. Because there was no way Bosworth

was going to get Untermyer to remove those greenhouses, he did what he could. As the main entrance, he designed an immense rectangular gate made of slabs of limestone—austere, even Egyptian in feeling—with the same diamond-scored panels as the walls. A panel above the gate displayed a beautiful relief of Artemis by sculptor Ulric H. Ellerhusen.

Inside the gate, the garden was revealed in spectacular fashion: a long canal stretched from the entryway to the north end, where the vista closed at the semicircular wall of the amphitheater. Halfway down the garden, another canal ran from east to west, forming a cross with the axial canal. Untermyer's canals were punctuated by "frequent water jets of varied design," in Bosworth's words, one of the jets terminating at its upper end in a broad basin before the theater. These cruciform canals are familiar elements, as he noted, throughout Persian and Mughal garden architecture; the Taj Mahal is one of the most famous. Two weeping willows were originally planted on each side of the canal at the entrance, framing the view. Later, these were replaced by weeping beeches, which grew to huge heights and made a magnificent canopy at the entrance.

Interestingly, Bosworth designed a not dissimilar Moorish garden at Kykuit. It has low instead of high walls, is also scored with a diamond pattern, and has a central canal with arching, Generalife-style jets of water at intervals. Bosworth likely saw how the Kykuit version could be expanded to create a far grander one for Untermyer.

The Greek influence made an appearance at the far end of this sweeping vista, where there was a small amphitheater, about 60 feet in diameter, with four rows of narrow stone seats arranged in a semicircle around a small stage. Behind the amphitheater was a semicircular limestone wall that framed the northern end, giving a soft curve to the otherwise geometric layout of the garden.

PREVIOUS PAGE Twin marble sphinxes watch over the Walled Garden from atop Ionic cipollino marble columns.

Flanking each side of the stage were two pairs of tall, Ionic columns made of cipollino marble, topped by marble sphinxes made by the most famous sculptor of the day, Paul Manship. Towering like benign guardians over the garden, the columns and sphinxes were reflected in the pool below, where the canal came to rest. The twin columns notably resembled those at the Boboli Gardens' Isolotto in Florence, Italy. Yet the sphinxes, often used in Greek funeral monuments, were similar to Attic figures dating from the sixth century BC. The embrace of different architectural styles displayed here shows Bosworth's willingness to combine Greek, Roman, and Islamic influences when the situation offered itself.

As at Kykuit, there was no fourth wall to this otherwise enclosed space. In a wise decision, Bosworth left the west side of the garden completely open to the breathtaking view down to the river and the Palisades. And here he was firmly in Greek mode. Instead of walls, he designed a circular colonnade which overlooked a large swimming pool. The colonnade, later called the Temple of the Sky, consisted of fourteen fluted Corinthian columns made of Alabama marble, about 30 feet in diameter. At their base, lions' heads carved by noted sculptor Frederick G. Roth spouted water into the pool. Through the columns, one could gaze in amazement at the panoramic vista spread out below. This see-through architectural feature mitigated the confining effect of the walls that constrained the rest of the garden, and Bosworth liked the results: he wrote appreciatively of the clouds moving above the columns. He also liked the steps on each side of the colonnade that led down to the pool, which reminded him "of the giant staircase between the Doge's Palace and St. Mark's, Venice." Here again, Bosworth acknowledges the Italian influence in his work. On both sides of the pool were parterres of mown grass, perfect for lawn parties. It is here that Isadora Duncan and her dancers performed for the Untermyers and their guests in the 1920s.

The floor of the colonnade was decorated with a circular mosaic in delicate pink, grey, and pale green hues, which also pleased Bosworth: "A Greek head of Medusa forms the center, surrounded by vines and

The Temple of the Sky features fourteen Corinthian columns and an elaborate
mosaic floor with the head of Medusa in the center.

various Greek ornaments in successive borders." He observed that the mosaic design "was of a gorgeous composition and beautifully executed." Bosworth loved mosaics. He lyrically described the black and white pebble mosaics and scallop shells decorating the swimming pool at Kykuit, and his passion for the mosaics in Untermyer's garden was just as enthusiastic. He pointed to the patterns in the bottom of Untermyer's swimming pool in poetic terms, extolling "great eccentric rings such as the rings that form on the surface when pebbles are dropped into the water, interspersed with crabs and fish, in mosaic; and on the walls of the pool at the surface of the water, the mosaic forms wave patterns."

Bosworth also singled out the superb mosaic on the stage of the amphitheater. It was taken from the wall decoration at Tiryns, "that famous piece of design featured in every history of art." The architect was moved to add, "All of the mosaics, of which there are many, show great care as to design and color and are a great adornment to the garden."

Bosworth's Achievement

Walking westward from the amphitheater, visitors passed under another colonnade of handsome Greek marble columns, leading to a narrow, unprepossessing doorway. And here could be found a good example of Bosworth's sense of the dramatic. Through this modest doorway, one beheld perhaps the most thrilling piece of architecture in the whole garden. It was aptly called the Vista—a long, wide flight of steps with landings, running down hundreds of feet toward the banks of the Hudson. The triumph of this part of the garden was what Untermyer had at his disposal, and what Rockefeller did not: some of the greatest natural scenery in the country. The Palisades—spectacular cliffs visible across the river—were different in appearance here than in other parts of the Hudson, more rugged and sculpted. They towered above the river like prehistoric figures carved into the cliff face, reminiscent of the monumental eroded pillars of

Bryce Canyon in Utah. At sunrise, these craggy rock formations, majestic and mysterious, glowed like fire, an unforgettable sight.

At the bottom of this stunning staircase, a circular terrace was punctuated by two great monolithic cipollino columns, some 30 feet high, brought from Europe by the late Stanford White. Bosworth may have acquired them from White's estate sale, which Untermyer attended. The columns rose up gracefully to the sky as if in answer to the dramatic

The original Vista offered a long staircase lined with cryptomeria, down to a terrace.
Two cipollino columns framed the view of the Hudson River and the Palisades.

One of the first features to be restored was the Vista. Note the low-lying Japanese forest grass replacing the long line of cryptomeria, so overgrown it blocked the view.

carved face of the Palisades. Bosworth conceded modestly that it was "an enchanting view."

Frank Untermyer, one of Samuel's grandsons, later said that according to his grandfather, the Vista derived from the famous Vista at the Villa D'Este on Lake Como. Side-by-side photographs of the two places confirm this striking similarity. It seems that, as with the staircases by the swimming pool, Bosworth couldn't resist slipping another Italianate element into his garden design. Beyond the Vista, at the river's edge, was a gatehouse guarded by statues of a lion and a unicorn, where visitors arriving by boat or walking from the railway station could enter the property.

The Vista's flight of steps acted like a dividing line between the mostly natural landscape bordered by the river to the west, and the open space to the north. Here Bosworth attempted to impose some discipline on the steeply sloping hillside. He created what later were called the Color Gardens, each flower bed dedicated to a specific color—blue, pink, yellow, red—and beyond them, the Rose and Dahlia Gardens. These could be accessed from the Vista staircase. More greenhouses and cold frames adjacent to the flower beds were included in the overall design. Farther north still, beyond these brilliant displays, were the Vegetable Gardens. A tennis court was installed to the north of the Walled Garden.

The final touch to this challenging site was, in Bosworth's opinion, "the unique feature of the place." Taming the land that lay outside the Rose Garden, he built a series of walled terraces of perfect formality and repetition. "Nothing is so refreshing as repetition in terracing of this kind, with the slight variety obtained by the difference in level." Stairways ran between the terrace walls, aligned with a little canal running down the middle and spilling through lions' heads into a stone basin on each landing. Turning farther toward the house, one saw an astonishing sight: a rocky cave set in the hillside, with the river as a backdrop. This theatrical feature was the work of Charles Davite, a Genoese rock gardener famous both in Europe and the United States. Around this cave, Davite created "an immense rock garden with caves and water-falls and basins, quite

Charles Davite created a stunning rock garden, "with caves and water-falls and basins . . ."

fantastic and marvellous [sic]." At the highest peak of this man-made caprice, a small rectangular Greek temple offered a delightful view over the rock garden with its streams and bridges and on down to the Hudson and the ever-thrilling Palisades.

Thomas H. Everett, the British-born director of multiple divisions of the New York Botanical Garden for decades and unofficial dean of American horticulture, acquired his first job in the United States as a gardener for Samuel Untermyer. Everett once said that the Greystone gardens were perhaps the finest example of a Beaux-Arts architectural garden ensemble in the country. Bosworth, whose work was not always greeted with enthusiasm by his fellow architects, must have appreciated this accolade.

Untermyer's Garden Artists

Bosworth, as well as being a talented landscape artist, was also a serious connoisseur of stonemasonry and sculpture. His appreciation of Charles Davite reflected his interest not only in the grounds of his gardens, but also in their three-dimensional decoration. Kykuit was full of grottoes and rocky streams and stone bridges. Fountains and statuary of all sorts were placed in strategic positions in John D. Rockefeller's garden.

It was owing to Bosworth's recommendations to Untermyer that several distinguished sculptors found a place in Untermyer's Yonkers garden. The most significant was Paul Manship, a young American who moved in 1905 from St. Paul, Minnesota, to New York City, and became an apprentice to the Viennese-born, Italian-trained Isidore Konti, a sculptor who lived, coincidentally, in Yonkers. At Konti's urging, Manship in 1909 applied for and won the Prix de Rome, which allowed him to live in Italy for three years. There, he immersed himself in the classical traditions of Rome and more particularly Greece, returning with an original, decorative style of sculpture that escaped from the École de Beaux-Arts straitjacket, yet provided a pleasingly stylized form of neoclassical art that offended nobody. Manship was modest about his success, saying, "I had no real talent, but was free and unencumbered. I was the right man at the right time."

Perhaps his most famous work was the 1930s gilded relief of Prometheus on the facade of the lower plaza of Rockefeller Center in New York City. When Bosworth, a friend of the sculptor, commissioned Manship in 1917 to make the two sphinxes that found themselves on top of the columns in the Walled Garden, Manship was probably already familiar with Untermyer's garden; his mentor Konti had earlier purchased a marble fountain figure called *The Brook* for Untermyer. Untermyer liked Manship's sphinxes enough to invite him to cast two bronze figures for the garden dramatizing the legend of Actaeon and Diana. Manship had already produced versions of these bronzes and shown them to great

Sculptor Paul Manship was brought on by Bosworth to create several pieces
for the Untermyer gardens, including the sphinxes.

acclaim in New York, where Untermyer might have seen them. In the myth, Actaeon, a hunter, by accident glimpses the chaste goddess Diana in her bath. In rage, Diana turns Actaeon into an animal and his pack of hounds, no longer recognizing their master, tears him to pieces. (Versions of the pair may be seen outside the Norton Museum of Art in West Palm Beach, Florida.) Manship's final versions for Untermyer were completed in 1925—two bronze statues, each four-and-a-half feet high, designed to complement each other in action from the myth. They were prominently displayed on each side of the amphitheater pool in the Walled Garden, where visitors could admire them while enjoying performances in the amphitheater.

Other well-known artists were brought in to decorate Untermyer's garden. Ulric Ellerhusen, who created the Artemis relief sculpture at the Walled Garden's entrance, was a German-American sculptor who came to the United States in 1894. After studying at the Art Institute of Chicago, he moved to New York, where he made a name for himself in architectural sculpture and relief work. Another important sculptor represented in the garden was Brooklyn-born Frederick G. Roth, who studied in Vienna and Berlin before returning to New York and quickly becoming a well-known animal sculptor in bronze. In 1906, the Metropolitan Museum of Art purchased five of his works, including a performing elephant that was very popular. The fine lions' heads spouting water at the base of the columns in the colonnade confirmed Bosworth's good taste in introducing Roth to Untermyer.

Perhaps the most intriguing of all the sculptures in Untermyer's garden was by a German artist, Walter Schott. Schott seems to have never come to America, living his life mostly in Berlin, where he did his major work. He died there, penniless, in 1938. Schott's chief patron was Kaiser Wilhelm, a relationship that lost Schott most of his commissions after World War I. But he left some fine pieces, including *Nymphenbruennen* (Three Dancing Maidens). In this Art Nouveau work, three graceful and animated figures dance in a circle around a jet of water that drenches them, causing their flimsy dresses to cling to their bodies. It is a bronze cast of this fountain, sitting on an elegantly sculpted base, that found its way to Untermyer's estate, where it took pride of place at the center of the circular driveway in front of the main house.

The original sculpture and four known copies remained in Europe. Schott is not known to have had exhibitions in New York, so it is unclear how either Bosworth or Untermyer first saw the work, but it was purchased directly from Schott's Berlin studio for Untermyer. The mystery remains, but so, fortunately, does the fountain. It is now called Untermyer Fountain, and is a prize ornament of New York's Conservatory Garden in Central Park, a gift of the Untermyer family after Samuel's death.

A bronze cast of sculptor Walter Schott's *Nymphenbruennen* once graced
the circular front driveway of Greystone. Today it is known as Untermyer Fountain
and located in New York's Central Park.

TOP German artist Walter Schott, seen here among his work, created the famed
Nymphenbruennen. ABOVE After its tenure in Untermyer's driveway, the
casting of Schott's *Nymphenbruennen* was moved to Central Park, New York.

The Architect and the Tree Hugger

Even with the impressive works of art and horticulture sprinkled throughout the landscape, those who visited Untermyer's estate found that one structure stood out above the rest: the high, crenellated walls that signaled the location of the Walled Garden. This place became the main focus—the part written about by reporters and admired by the thousands of guests who passed through the tall gateway, meandered past the canals, sat down in the amphitheater, wandered in and out of the colonnaded temple, and gasped at the Vista every year from around 1920 on. The Walled Garden was featured in several architectural journals shortly after it opened, and popular magazines continued to show it to their readers, many of whom had probably never before seen a walled garden with canals, let alone an amphitheater.

A few years after the completion of the Walled Garden, Julia Morgan, the first woman to be accepted at the École des Beaux-Arts, delivered up an elaborately colonnaded and mosaic-lined swimming pool for William Randolph Hearst in San Simeon, his enormous estate in California. The pool became the focal point of Hearst's garden, and, along with Bosworth's structures for Untermyer at Greystone, represented perhaps the apotheosis of the classical style of landscape design in North America—as well as evidence of the tenacious authority of the École des Beaux-Arts. Perhaps this was not coincidence. Hearst and Untermyer knew each other quite well; they visited one another in Palm Beach, and in 1918, Untermyer represented Hearst's newspaper empire in a copyright lawsuit. Perhaps on their vacations in Florida they talked about their swimming pools.

Bosworth had only one criticism of the layout of his magnificent terraces and waterworks. "The chief defect of the formal gardens seems to be the absence of a canal on the lower terrace," he wrote in his essay in *The Architectural Review*, "which is somewhat meaningless without it." In explanation, he said that "the owner [Untermyer is never mentioned in the article by name] as we are informed could not bring himself to

Architect Charles Wellford Leavitt Jr. drew up plans for a water pipe system that would serve many of the gardens' canals and pools.

the point of executing this canal because it necessitated the removal of a tree." A perfect example of the difference between Untermyer and his designer—one, an artist, longing for a canal to complete the symmetry of his garden plan; the other, a tree hugger, determined to protect the natural elements of the land, even if they spoiled the artist's vision.

There is evidence that other important architects worked on the garden, in particular Charles Wellford Leavitt Jr. Leavitt was described as a "landscape engineer," with special knowledge of Egyptian architecture and landscapes; his work for the mausoleum of Julius Bache in Woodlawn was widely admired. He also did work for the parklike landscape in Somerville, New Jersey, belonging to James Buchanan Duke, Doris's father. Two surviving plans drawn up for Untermyer in the fall of 1916 by Leavitt show an elaborate water pipe system designed for the canals and pools in several of the gardens.

Over the years, changes continued to be made to the layout of the gardens. No doubt to Bosworth's delight, the Tilden greenhouses were removed by 1922, thus allowing for a path to be built directly from the mansion to the Walled Garden, creating a far better introduction to its crenellated walls and massive entrance gate. The rock gardens were continually expanded. Sculptures were added.

But with Minnie's untimely death in 1924, the poetry readings and concerts stopped, and the importance of the amphitheater and colonnades diminished. Untermyer, missing his wife's presence in these theatrical spaces, turned away from architecture, focusing his energies on his deepest interests, the flowers, fruit, and vegetables he produced in his gardens and greenhouses. No new buildings were constructed on the property after 1924.

As for Bosworth, the timing of Untermyer's changed focus was fortuitous. In 1924, John D. Rockefeller Jr., son of Bosworth's most important client and a good friend, started a fund to help restore some of France's major monuments that had become neglected after World War I. Rockefeller asked the family's trusted architect to head the project, which included the Palace of Versailles, the Château de Fontainebleau and Notre-Dame de Reims. Bosworth, who had already taken on several commissions outside the United States, became a permanent resident of France, built a house there for his family, and remained there for the rest of his life.

Bosworth's place in American architectural history is probably secure, despite so much of his career taking place abroad. He is best known for his Beaux-Arts designs for the Cambridge campus of Massachusetts Institute of Technology, the former AT&T Building in New York, and Kykuit. He is also credited with over half of the elegant bridges built for John D. Rockefeller Jr. over the carriage trails on Mount Desert Island, Maine (which can still be admired in what is now Acadia National Park). Many of his other buildings are lost, including a huge mansion for the Rockefellers, which, at the time, was the tallest single-family home in New York.

Yet he had a problematic career in America. He never worked in a partnership, unusual for an architect of his time. He had unconventional

In 1924, John D. Rockefeller Jr. asked his friend Bosworth to manage a project in France, which coincided with Samuel Untermyer's shift in focus from garden design to plants.

opinions, such as that architects were artists, not engineers (as was evident in his calling on Leavitt to do the structural work at Greystone), and that therefore, as he said in an address to students at Columbia, "one's creation is an exact expression of himself!" He was also perhaps too devoted to the dictates of the beaux arts, and failed to move with his contemporaries into the modern age. He had a faddish interest in physical health, urging his students to "develop a healthy, vigorous body." He applied three times to become a Fellow of the American Institute of Architects, admittedly the most exclusive of clubs, and three times he was rejected. The reasons were opaque, but there were unpleasant references to "dirty work," and "discrediting the competence of the profession." On his fourth try, in 1950, he was finally accepted, at the age of almost 82.

Bosworth's life in Paris was rather more fun than it had been at home. In addition to the restoration of some of France's most famous monuments, interesting projects for Rockefeller included the purchase of the Unicorn Tapestries (now at the Cloisters in New York), which Bosworth kept in his vault for several weeks after their arrival in the United States because of customs issues. Also thanks to Rockefeller, Bosworth was

In addition to Untermyer Gardens, Bosworth's notable works include the Cambridge, Massachusetts, campus of the Massachusetts Institute of Technology.

catapulted into the glamorous world of Tutankhamun and the English archeologist Howard Carter, who in 1922 had made the sensational discovery of the pharaoh's tomb in Egypt. Rockefeller was thinking of funding a new antiquities museum in Cairo, and Bosworth went to King Tut's tomb in 1925 to meet Carter. Carter was not particularly welcoming (Carter's employer, the fifth Earl of Carnarvon, was an impetuous and temperamental character who demanded Carter's full-time attention cataloging the tomb's treasures), but the two became friends and in the 1930s worked together in Paris on a slightly fishy deal that culminated in the sale of two Egyptian statues to the Metropolitan Museum of Art. (Both Bosworth and Carter were eager to avoid paying taxes on the sale.)

The friendship between Bosworth and Carter lasted until the latter's death in 1939. Bosworth appreciated Carter's rather eccentric sense of humor, and they shared the experience of having worked for two very rich and demanding clients.

It is not known if Bosworth ever went back to Untermyer's garden, which of course changed immeasurably after his departure. The architect died in Paris in 1966 at the age of 97.

Untermyer Estate, 1907

1. Greystone Mansion
2. Carriage House
3. Greenhouses
4. Gatehouse
5. Hudson River

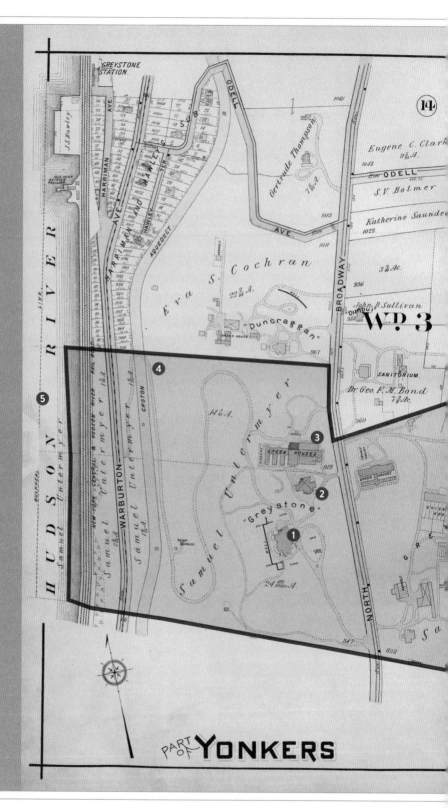

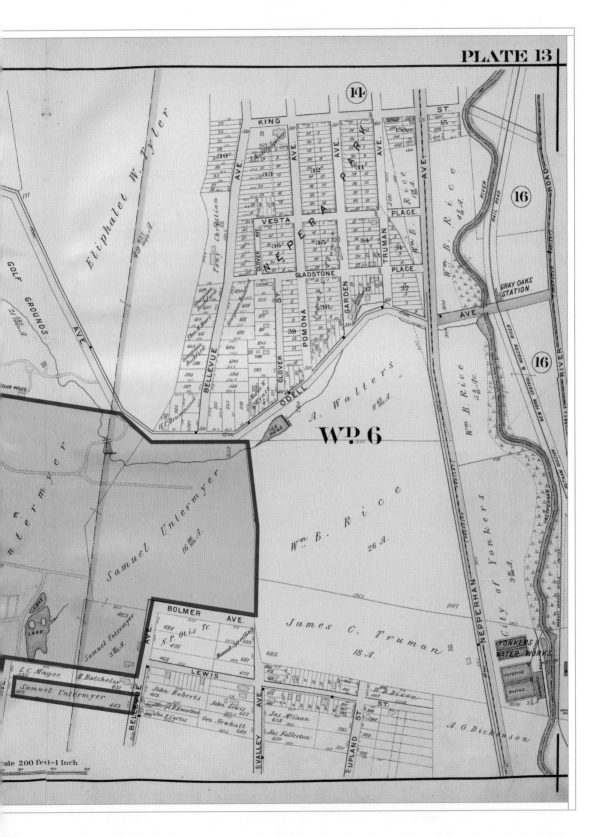

PLATE 13

WD 6

Scale 200 feet—1 Inch

The
HORTICULTURE

"I'd rather look at flowers
than at a great painting or listen
to great organ music."

—SAMUEL UNTERMYER

Preparing the Ground

Untermyer's architect Welles Bosworth understood from the start that his client's top priority was not the elegant temples or delightful rockeries that Bosworth had in mind for him, but the flowers, plants, trees, and shrubs that would grow in the vast landscape delivered to his care. Never mind. Bosworth went ahead anyway with his Islamic waterways, Italianate stairways, Greek columns, statuary, mosaics, rock formations, and winding pathways—to spectacular effect.

Yet while Bosworth was first and foremost an architect, he had done enough garden design by this time, particularly for the Rockefellers at Kykuit, to understand how to incorporate an exterior planting plan in a way that Untermyer would find acceptable. The architect's most obvious contribution was, according to his employer, the plantings in and around Bosworth's personal triumph, the Walled Garden. Though little documented, these additions consisted mostly of simple bedding plants lining the canals, along with low-growing perennials and the two fine beech (originally willow) trees inside the entrance gate.

Whether Bosworth also oversaw the planning of the flower gardens that ultimately became the most famous aspect of Untermyer's glamorous estate is not clear. In Bosworth's article for *The Architectural Review*, which is mostly devoted to the architectural wonders he devised for Untermyer, he briefly refers to these gardens as "dedicated to all sorts of flower schemes and color schemes. There are tulip gardens, blue gardens, pink gardens, yellow gardens of varying sizes and designs . . ." At the end of the series, parallel to the river, was the Rose Garden.

He continues, "Passing through this one reaches perhaps the unique feature of the place. It is a series of walled terraces of perfect formality similar to its neighbor and delightfully repetitive." He goes on to describe

One of Bosworth's Italianate fences, running alongside a luscious border
of flowers and shrubs.

small staircases in between the walls, "paralleling a little canal running
down the middle and spilling through lions' heads into a stone basin on
each landing." At the top of this terraced hillside was the great rock cave
and gardens designed by Charles Davite, "quite fantastic and marvellous
[sic]." The reader can have no doubt from these enthusiastic passages
where Welles Bosworth's loyalties lay. So much for the flower gardens.
He clearly was not interested in specifying any particular species or type
of flower. But someone was.

Flowers Bloom at Greystone

In 1900, it was announced in a British horticultural trade journal that
W. H. Waite, foreman of the herbaceous garden at the Royal Botanic Garden Edinburgh, was going to work in America for Samuel Untermyer.

How Untermyer found him is not known, but this British import was an inspired hire.

William Henry Waite was born in 1873. Little is known about his early career, but as he was only 27 when he took the job with Untermyer, he must have started gardening at a young age. Once at Greystone, he soon showed his talents, not only as a knowledgeable horticulturalist, but also as a brilliant cultivator and propagator of plants. A year after he arrived, bids were being invited from nurserymen across the country to acquire 30,000 trees, shrubs, and plants—including 1500 roses. Waite most certainly meant business. And his employer was happy to indulge him.

By 1913, Waite was regularly winning prizes for Untermyer at flower shows, and getting both his and his employer's names in the papers. In an annual fall flower show of the Horticultural Society of New York, Waite's bush chrysanthemum plants attracted much attention, as did his trained specimen single chrysanthemum that was shaped like a fan. He was a magician with cattleya orchids. Another specialty was dahlias, about which he wrote a catalog and, later, a book. Orchids and dahlias were Untermyer's favorites, so needless to say, Waite's employer was delighted at these triumphs. They once again proved his ability to win at whatever he put his hand to.

Once Waite became superintendent of the Greystone gardens, and as the prizes mounted and tourists clamored to see the floral spectacles, all was smooth between employer and his hard-working chief of staff. In 1919, Untermyer embarked on an extension of the greenhouses, adding three peach houses, two plant houses, a grape house, an office building, and a residence for the help. By 1922, gardens had also been planned for commercial use—chicken and poultry houses, a carpentry and paint shop, dog kennel, and stable. More housing was built for the staff required to manage the constantly expanding property. Waite's success was such that he started his own nursery business and began to acquire his own clients.

Untermyer spent on one occasion more than $20,000 importing the best rhododendrons from England. A 1921 story in the *New York Times*

The neat rows of the Color and Vegetable Gardens, with Bosworth's pavilions, stretching almost as far as the eye can see along the property.

stated that Untermyer's gardens cost him $1 million (over $14 million in today's money). This was an exceptional sum in the gardening world, and people began to take notice. Descriptions of Greystone began to appear regularly in the press, both nationally and internationally, sometimes with surprising facts. A reporter for the British tabloid the *Daily Express* announced to his unsuspecting readers that Untermyer's garden in Yonkers was "an exact reproduction of Hampton Court." Another equally inaccurate but thrilling news item was that Untermyer once grew the largest chrysanthemum in the world. "It was seven feet high, sixteen feet across, and bore 2,000 blossoms!" (Untermyer refrained from correcting the reporter's flight of fancy, no doubt aware that the owner of the newspaper where these stories ran was the controversial and disputatious press mogul, Lord Beaverbrook. The two men were not unalike; on occasion Beaverbrook visited Untermyer at The Willows.)

An early photograph of the rock garden, with flowers and small trees in abundance.

While many of the original trees have disappeared, flowers still play a leading role in the restored rock garden beneath the Temple of Love.

In September 1927, Gove Hambidge, a reporter for *Better Homes and Gardens*, visited and gave a detailed description of how Untermyer was spending his money. Hambidge was an excellent choice for the assignment. Unlike the *Daily Express* reporter, he happened to be a knowledgeable botanist, and on his visit to Greystone, he walked through the gardens with keen interest, identifying an impressive list of plants that confirmed his already high opinion of Mr. Untermyer. Hambidge wrote of the Color Gardens:

> . . . because it will be of practical interest to other amateur gardeners, I am going to list at least some of the flowers Mr. Untermyer named as growing here. In the pink garden: annual asters, verbena, snapdragon,

Some of the 60 gardeners employed by Untermyer,
in front of the similarly numerous greenhouses.

phlox . . . hollyhock, gladiolus, clarkia, veronica, chrysanthemum. In the blue garden: forget-me-not, heliotrope, torenia, petunia, globe thistle, salvia, scabiosa, monkshood, ageratum, delphinium, anchusa. In the red garden: gladiolus, geranium, begonia, penstemon, fuchsia, canna. In the white garden: . . . meadow sweet, Japanese and German iris, marguerite, lantana, verbena, sweet william. In the yellow garden: lantana, calendula, chrysanthemum, coreopsis, canna, mimulus.

As Untermyer made clear to his guest, the magnificent displays in the Color Gardens, growing in plots punctuated by Bosworth's terraces, stairways, fountains, and pergolas, were precisely what he, Samuel Untermyer, had envisioned. In this respect, he was reflecting the new passion in Europe for flowers, as was emphasized by the flood of brilliant paintings of gardens produced by impressionist and post-impressionist

Delphiniums were a mainstay of the blue Color Garden,
and a favorite of Untermyer's.

painters such as Monet, Bonnard, Fantin-Latour, Redon, and others. "I have a love of rich color," he declared, "and I want as much of it around me as possible." Moreover, he knew his public, and his public loved the flower gardens, too—the more dazzling, the better.

His ambition required more, however, than the exuberant displays in the Color Gardens. Every spring, he planted thousands of bulbs throughout the estate. "Fifty thousand bulbs, a riot of color," he boasted in Hambidge's story. "And for harmony or contrast, spread beneath them like a velvet carpet, fifty thousand rich-textured pansies. Can you imagine what a sight that is?" Most people couldn't. But he didn't stop there. What about the rhododendrons, Untermyer's pride and joy? Rose-pink, yellow, white, lilac, purple! Thirty thousand rhododendrons of all colors bloomed every year in Samuel Untermyer's garden.

Naturally, all these stunning horticultural miracles did not appear as if by magic out of the ground. Untermyer would have thought less of them if they did. He, after all, was famous for loving a fight. This one, however, did not take place in the courtroom. Here he was facing a more mercurial antagonist, going head to head with Mother Nature. "It is ungrateful soil, thin and stony," Untermyer observed of his property. "I have had to make a good deal of it myself so that it would be more friendly and nutritious. I have blasted out rock, and in many places mixed large quantities of peat into the topsoil—a thousand tons of it at least."

Untermyer paid serious attention to each plant and how he would use it. For instance, he bought six boxwood specimens, perhaps 100 years old, to line a path leading to the house. His boxwood collection alone was probably worth $25,000, and for these new ones, no expense was spared. They were of an English variety, with the smaller leaves that Untermyer favored. They were also rugged, not manicured or topiaried like most boxwoods preferred by Americans. "A boxwood tree is like a man," he explained, "more interesting if not too smooth. The pruning shears should yield to the contours of natural growth."

Learning the science of horticulture, he experimented with old varieties and new ones just appearing on the market. "I like to go into the greenhouse with a brush or a rabbit's foot, carefully transfer pollen from the stamens of one variety of flower to the pistil of another, and see what comes of the cross." He had produced a hybrid delphinium and a beautiful salmon-colored salvia in this manner. (No other garden owners of Untermyer's wealth and social position would have been caught dead holding a trowel in their hands.) Not only flowers, but also rare tropical species and varieties of fruits and vegetables flourished under Untermyer's careful tutelage. Melons and vegetables in winter, dwarf peaches, grapes, nectarines, figs, and of course orchids—thousands of them—all responded to his guidance in the greenhouses Bosworth had so longed to remove. Untermyer loved eating his exotic fruits out of season, and confessed that he would like to do a good deal more of this kind of experimenting than he had time for.

Early color images couldn't capture the brilliant hues of the flower displays.

Sometimes he spoke of his flowers as though they were his offspring. In explaining how much straw manure he had to import into the garden (twelve hundred tons a year), he explained, "You have to feed plants, like humans, plenty of nourishing food if you expect them to grow up healthy and vigorous." One is hard put to find a remark of Untermyer's concerning his three children, Alvin, Irwin, and Irene, that expresses quite the same affection.

Untermyer valued the orchid above all other flowers,
and the odontioda above all other orchids.

He told Hambidge that his three favorite flowers were the delphinium,
the dahlia, and the orchid. But the one he loved above all was the orchid.
"The orchid is the king of flowers," he declared, "because it is superior
to all other flowers in beauty of shape and color, in delicacy and aesthetic
appeal, and because it is most difficult to cultivate."

He liked to compare his gardening to the fine arts. He recognized
that his passion was mostly aesthetic, similar to the contemplation of
paintings. He said once that it was akin to the weaving of rich tapestries
or the painting of mural decorations. "But in gardening, one can work on

so much larger a scale than in any other art except possibly architecture." These are not the ramblings of a dilettante, but the musings of an artist. As he looked around at all the spectacular plants he had brought into being, he said, "Such things give me the thrill of music played on a great organ."

Samuel Untermyer had earned his gardening chops honorably. He had come to gardening as a student and honed his knowledge over the years. He had traveled widely with Minnie to gardens in Europe and England, as well as all over the United States. As with any project he undertook, he read, studied, experimented, and got his hands dirty for the purpose of understanding as thoroughly as possible what was at stake. So when Samuel Untermyer asserted to Hambidge that apart from the Walled Garden, he himself laid out the grounds and gardens, Hambidge saw no reason to doubt him. (Welles Bosworth was by this time living in France, and thus unavailable to dispute his former client's claim.)

It is interesting to read Hambidge's impressions at the end of his autumn visit to Greystone. After all, he had the eye of a professional. What Hambidge found particularly charming was the way Untermyer trained and pruned his shrubs, such as the forsythia and the English ivy. He pointed with approval to the occasional gnarled apple tree left on the lawn as a genuinely picturesque and valuable part of the landscape. He noted the numbers of birds that regarded Greystone as a sanctuary. "As it now must be clear," he concluded, "Mr. Untermyer is wealthy enough to indulge his hobby on the most extensive scale. But what an essentially wholesome, normal, satisfying and infinitely varied hobby it is—passion rather, in his case . . . If anything would make me desirous of assuming the burden of wealth (a game, as I believe, not often worth the candle), it would be that I too might create some such place of deep delight in this gardener's paradise."

In 1919, Untermyer declared that the Magnolia Gardens in Charleston, South Carolina, with their giant azaleas in full bloom and their wonderful magnolias and live oaks, was "the finest garden to be found anywhere in the world—barring none—and I have seen most of them."

Untermyer proclaimed Magnolia Gardens, in Charleston, South Carolina, "the finest garden . . . in the world" in 1919, though many would come to say the same about his garden only a few years later.

The Magnolia Gardens, now known as Magnolia Plantation and Gardens, were opened to the public in 1870. When Samuel Untermyer opened his Greystone estate to the public about 50 years later, with its 60 gardeners and 60 greenhouses, he might have amended his statement about the Magnolia Gardens. In many people's eyes at that point, his own garden topped them all.

Trouble in Paradise

But dark clouds gradually began to gather over the Greystone gardens. Waite encouraged Untermyer to spend more and more profligately on the gardens and Untermyer finally began to chafe at the astronomical bills he was receiving. While Waite grew frustrated at his boss's resistance, Untermyer increasingly complained about mismanagement, and by 1930, the two men were barely on speaking terms. Here is part of a typical weekly report Waite sent to Untermyer at that time: "During the past week the lawns were all reseeded and the new lawn in the Greek Garden, also the lawn at Woodlawn [where Minnie was buried]. Nearly all the spring planting has been done in the various gardens." He goes on to explain that there was not sufficient preparation to plant the Color Gardens with perennials "to keep up the constant show of color necessary." Perennials, he points out, would also have saved money on the annuals, "which naturally keep the expenses of Greystone very high." He regrets the poor show of Easter plants in the greenhouses, which was also caused by the lack of proper preparation. "You should have had at least a whole house of rambler roses now in bloom, instead of three or four of the miserable specimens you have."

Waite constantly complained about supply problems. "The other day I ordered the Boxwoods sprayed for the mite. There is only about three days in the whole year that this is effective, as they should be sprayed as soon as the insects emerge. They could not be sprayed as we had to get an estimate on Molasses." (Molasses spray was long believed to be a deterrent to insect pests.) Again, "After the hot spell we had recently, I noticed that the climbing roses were suffering with red spider and ordered them sprayed immediately. We did not have enough plant spray to go round." Then there were staff issues. A ploughman was needed in the Vegetable Gardens and a man was hired by an assistant named Clunas. Untermyer said the new worker should have done in one day what it took him three to accomplish. "Surely Clunas or I ought to be the better judge of that," Waite responded testily, "and if we are not, then it is fully time you had another superintendent."

Waite was a perfectionist, and he was beginning to see that Untermyer was losing a little of the intensity that he had shown during the first years of the garden. Waite despised Untermyer's quibbling over the bills, and he sensed that the organization he had so carefully put together over the years was falling apart. When Untermyer complained that "everything is topsy turvy," Waite was furious, telling Untermyer he had been trying to correct this, but that they had 58 people on the payroll, of whom 29 were daily men, and very few were gardeners, "far too few for Greystone." The theme became a drumbeat. "I thought I had everything working smoothly," Waite wrote, "when instructions from you upset everything again." The final alarm for Waite sounded when a rival, George H. Chisholm, arrived at Greystone in 1928 to work for Untermyer. Waite's long working agreement with Untermyer was poised to unravel.

A letter from Waite to Untermyer in May 1930 reveals the disintegration of their relationship. It lists a litany of complaints about plant diseases, staff issues, damaging purchasing delays, even the failure of Untermyer to pay for delivery of 500 dahlias "easily valued at $2,000." Finally, he writes, "I have decided not to come to Greystone any more as I am entirely too busy with my own business to waste time at Greystone, which seems to me to be utterly futile . . . In view of all these things and many others it shows me how hopeless is any attempt that I may make to help you with Greystone, as I have said it is simply a waste of my time and your money." After additional bitter remarks, he ends by stating, "I regret that I am leaving you so abruptly but I am so discouraged that I can not continue any longer."

Untermyer's immediate response? A brief, terse telegram: DON'T BE FOOLISH. EVIDENTLY A MISUNDERSTANDING.

But on this occasion, Untermyer's legendary skill at negotiation failed to impress. Waite had seen the writing on the wall. He kept his word and parted company with Untermyer for his own nursery in Eatontown, New Jersey, leaving Greystone in the hands of another British import with even more impressive credentials than Waite's had been.

The Last Partnership

George H. Chisholm was a Welshman who learned his horticulture at the University of Wales. One of his early assignments from the British government was to study plant disease among lilies in Bermuda. After moving to the United States in the late 1920s, he attracted clients such as William Rockefeller, Andrew Carnegie, and Nicholas Brady. But perhaps his most significant client from a career standpoint was the Duchess of Talleyrand, the former heiress Anna Gould, who had a famous collection of orchids growing in greenhouses at her Tarrytown, New York, estate. *Orchids*! Untermyer saw at once that he must have Chisholm for himself.

Their first encounter had not been promising. According to Geoffrey Hellman in the *New Yorker*, Chisholm first met Untermyer in 1928 in order to sell him a rock garden. Untermyer pretended to be outraged. "Have you seen my rock garden?" he asked. "It's a geological monstrosity," Chisholm responded. This was just the kind of riposte Untermyer enjoyed, and two years later he hired Chisholm and purchased his rock garden. The two became contentious and happy garden partners until the end of Untermyer's life.

Unlike Waite, who was always frustrated by Untermyer's stubbornness over bills, Chisholm seemed to quickly ferret out his employer's weakness, persuading Untermyer that money should be no object if he wanted the biggest camellia in the world, or for a rare 10-foot-high fern to win first prize in the next flower show. How could Untermyer resist such a challenge? He found it impossible to say no to Chisholm—even when Chisholm went so far as to experiment with inoculating honeydew melon vines with cognac, port, and Benedictine liqueurs. The spiked-fruit experiment went nowhere, but delighted Untermyer with its creativity and publicity value.

Another Chisholm contribution was the living sundial, a 36-foot, circular flower bed with the numbered hours planted in different colored plants. It was opened to the public in May 1937. Chisholm declared that

One of George Chisolm's contributions to the gardens was a giant floral sundial that he assured Untermyer could reliably tell time.

with careful study, one could tell the correct time within five or six minutes. He also enjoyed surprising his master with horticultural novelties, such as creating umbrellas, fans, swans, and canoes out of flowers. In one case, he produced a life-sized boat made of yellow cascade chrysanthemums. The boat "floated" in a pond of mountain laurel. A life-size Native American was in the boat, wielding a paddle; both the figure and the oar were also made of chrysanthemums.

Perhaps Chisholm's greatest tour de force was a model of Notre Dame, eight feet high, containing electric lights, chimes, and 36 windows painted to resemble stained glass, which won a gold medal at the Museum of Natural History in 1939 as "the best chrysanthemum Notre Dame on the premises."

Chisholm oversaw the addition of the Temple of Love to the rock garden.

What fun the two garden fanatics must have had! Untermyer enjoyed Chisholm's floral surprises and horticultural creativity, but perhaps more important, he respected his manager's botanical knowledge. The respect was mutual. Chisholm recalled that one day Untermyer, feeling the texture of a young plant's leaves, said, "You're not going to have very good chrysanthemums this year." He was right. Chisholm once said that Untermyer knew more Latin names than he did. They would argue about botanical terms, and Untermyer would try to catch his manager out, but according to Chisholm, he never succeeded. Chisholm's genius was that he knew how to stand up to Untermyer as few people could. Untermyer loved it.

The intricate iron cupola at the top of the Temple of Love.

When Untermyer grew ill and started spending more and more time in Palm Springs, Chisholm held the fort and continued to develop the garden. A temple to give a focal point to the rock garden, consisting of six delicate columns and a lacy iron cupola, was imported from France and called the Temple of Love. According to Chisholm, Untermyer liked taking a nap there. In 1937, the garden borders were planted with 250,000 tulips, maintaining the kind of brilliant display the visitors—and Untermyer—demanded. But perhaps Chisholm's most valuable duty was to nurse along the 4000 orchids in the orchid house, in particular the odontiodas, which had to be kept in tip-top shape every day so that one could grace Untermyer's lapel.

An abbreviated sample of the plant inventories for those years shows the astonishing extent of the collections and varieties of species under Chisholm's guardianship:

Inventory of Orchids, 1936.

Over 3200 orchids, including 1400 species of cattleya, over 700 odontiodas, 166 dendrobiums, and 207 phalaenopsis.

Plant Lists for Sale, 1938.*

4000 poinsettias	1200 tuberose begonias
6000 chrysanthemums	1000 celosias

---

* (Every year, Untermyer would put up certain of his plant material for sale, supposedly to bolster the ever-expanding expenses of the garden.)

Plants Ordered for Spring Planting, 1939.

20,000 pansies	10,000 sweet william
11,000 campanula	6000 primula
1000 myosotis	7500 phlox
2500 hollyhocks	4750 digitalis

Approximately 58,000 perennials for field and frames, including:

6000 asters	8500 rock plants
15,5000 hardy chrysanthemums of over 50 different species	15,000 border perennials such as aquilegia, dicentra, veronica, physostegia, primula
3000 iris germanica	

Plants in field: 76,000.

Another early color photo captures a quiet resting spot in Untermyer Gardens, with flowers, shrubs, small trees, a statue, and stone benches.

When Untermyer died, Chisholm had to oversee the closing of the property, assembling a complete list of all plants and flowers in the garden and the greenhouses. All would go up for sale at Parke-Bernet auction gallery and other horticultural sales events. As well as being enormously difficult, this task must have also been bittersweet. Chisholm was, however, philosophical about his employer's demise, saying he hoped to stay on as manager of the greenhouses and perhaps later as landscaper for the contemplated real estate development of the property.

Chisholm's last act of devotion after Untermyer's death was to replant the plot in the cemetery garden at Woodlawn where Minnie was waiting for her husband. "I laid out a $36,000 plot for him," he said, "with 150 rhododendron trees, over one and a half acres. Bigger than Carnegie's," he added slyly, knowing that that detail was what Untermyer would have

Hydrangeas bloom in one of the 60 greenhouses that could once be found on the Untermyer property.

liked best. Chisholm completed his duties in exemplary style. For some time afterward, he continued to visit and maintain the plot that he had laid out for his late employer.

Twelve years after Samuel Untermyer's death, George Chisholm died in Yonkers General Hospital, not far from Greystone. He was 65 years old, and left a wife, a daughter, a brother, and a sister.

There's little doubt that his life after Untermyer lost its flavor. The relationship between the two men was unique, quite outside the usual form of employer and employee. Each understood the other's foibles, each enjoyed the other's sense of humor, and each respected the other's wide and deep knowledge of horticulture, their joint passion. It would not be farfetched to say that Untermyer's life was extended by the presence of Chisholm, and Chisholm replaced the family that Untermyer had largely sacrificed to his work. The wonderful gardens they nurtured together are lasting proof of the successful partnership they conducted at Greystone for over a decade.

The

TRIUMPH

"One of the showplaces of America."

—PHILADELPHIA ENQUIRER, FEBRUARY 5, 1924

In 1922, Edith Wharton published her masterpiece, *The Age of Innocence*, which looked back to the 1880s, when New York was changing rapidly from a sedate, patrician city governed by old money to an unregulated new world of entrepreneurs and immigrants, a world where people like Samuel Untermyer thrived. She describes the clash between the old upper-middle-class families who lived in brownstones ("of which the uniform hue coated New York like a cold chocolate sauce") in Washington Square and Gramercy Park, and the new breed of nouveau riche millionaires who built vast chateaus and palazzos (with ballrooms) along Fifth Avenue and farther north, who had children out of wedlock, and who brandished their wealth in the face of the disapproving old guard.

In Wharton's book, Jews belonged to the latter crowd, and she showed how the old WASP tribes both feared and respected these clever, iconoclastic characters who were turning the established traditions upside down. Wharton denied the often-repeated rumor that Julius Montfort in *The Age of Innocence* was based on August Belmont, the real-life Jewish banker, racing aficionado, and patron of the arts. But the inference stuck. Montfort, with his worldly, "foreign" ways, represented to Wharton's readers all the dangers and ambitions that were threatening the stability of the ruling families of Old New York.

Samuel Untermyer could have been a model for one of Wharton's characters. He fit the profile perfectly, and his definitive contribution to the new world she describes was his park and gardens at Greystone. He had already become a household word in New York's legal circles. "Samuel Untermyer has been landing on the front pages for almost 40 years quite

Following the lead of many prominent figures of the time, Samuel and Minnie Untermyer had their portraits created. This likeness of Minnie by American portraitist James Jebusa Shannon was completed in 1906.

unaided," wrote Pulitzer Prize–winning author Henry F. Pringle in his book, *Big Frogs*. "His name has been in the headlines thousands of times."

As people began to recognize him from the countless photographs in the newspapers, Untermyer did what other arrivistes did and had a proper portrait created of himself. The artist was Anders Zorn, a Swedish portraitist popular at the time, who painted three American presidents as well as financiers and socialites. Minnie Untermyer had her portrait painted too, first by the German salon painter Conrad Kiesel in 1894, then a much grander one by the well-known American, James Jebusa Shannon. Today one might expect a power couple like the Untermyers to have chosen for their likenesses the biggest star of the time, John Singer Sargent, whose virtuoso portraits (including those of John D. Rockefeller and Woodrow Wilson) have overshadowed those of his contemporaries. But by the early twentieth century, Sargent had acquired a mixed reputation—his provocative portrait of Madame X had caused a major scandal—and he had announced he was giving up society portraiture. He even turned down J. P. Morgan, which must have tickled Untermyer no end.

But with the opening of the gardens at Greystone, a whole new wave of publicity attached to the celebrity lawyer, and this time he shared the spotlight with his wife. Minnie was in her prime during these Greystone years. She was described at the time by poet Jean Starr Untermeyer (no relation; different spelling) as "a pretty woman of medium height and weight, with beautiful white hair, a bright complexion, and a voice high and bell-like that suggested to me the tones of the celesta." Minnie complemented her husband's horticultural ambitions with her own philanthropic ones. Focusing on music, her chief passion, she became deeply committed to the New York Philharmonic Orchestra (as it was originally called). In 1909, she assembled a group of wealthy New York wives to help put the orchestra on a more secure financial footing, and, causing a stir in the music world that still resonates today, helped bring Gustav Mahler, the controversial Jewish conductor and composer, from Berlin to New York as music director. Minnie conceded it was a "big undertaking." Mahler

Minnie was instrumental in bringing famed German conductor Gustav Mahler, seen here circa 1909, to the New York Philharmonic Orchestra as music director.

conducted there from 1909 to 1911 (he died later that year). There were many tensions between the conductor and the women on the committee, mostly over money and contracts. Alma Mahler in her memoir said that Minnie was the only exception, and that Gustav called her his guardian angel. "A thousand thanks and our love, undying love," he and Alma wrote to her on their final return to Germany. "You are the only person who makes leaving difficult for us. We embrace you."

Although it seems Mahler never went to Greystone, many other famous musicians did. Called "an amusing little opera," Mozart's *The Impresario* was performed at Greystone in May 1922 before 300 guests, with the Philharmonic's celebrated guest conductor, Willem Mengelberg, in charge. The press, as usual in rapt attendance, noted the charm of the little theater, with its terraces for seats, silk draperies for background, and the tulip gardens in full bloom behind the garden walls.

In this idyllic spot, Minnie, called "the queen of the afternoon," held poetry readings and recitals by distinguished visiting artists. Such events became the pinnacle of the summer season. Dancers pranced on the lawn below the colonnade, and the amphitheater, just as Untermyer (and Welles Bosworth) had envisioned it, became a prize venue for cultural programs, its architectural elegance and mosaic decoration enhancing whatever artistic endeavors were performed there. The artworks and sculptures that Untermyer had collected over the years, mostly on Bosworth's advice, were another highlight of the visitors' experience. In those heady spring and summer days, Untermyer's dream was fulfilled, that $14 million (and counting) worth every penny.

Destination: Greystone

Many contemporary press descriptions confirm the success of Untermyer's ambitions for his garden. The attractions were on a scale not seen in other estates opened to the public at that time, and most of the other wealthy landowners with great gardens in the area did not have Untermyer's flair for publicity, honed during his years at the bar. Every detail was carefully calibrated. Guests usually traveled by private cars or on a special train from Grand Central Station, and the reception upon their arrival was always delightful. As the *New York Times* reported, "The house was decorated with dogwood blossoms, orchids and roses (from the Untermyer conservatory). Mrs. Untermyer in a costume of white chiffon and lace, received the guests."

The drawing room at Greystone was ideal for welcoming guests from around the world.

On one occasion, tea was served on the terrace, where the Kneisel Quartet performed Schubert and Beethoven. At another event, the tables were decorated with Easter lilies, 'American Beauty' roses and flowering plants from the conservatories, to the delight of the Astors, Lehmans, and several ambassadors who were in attendance.

It wasn't all highbrow. There were constant visits from garden clubs, flower shows for children, and benefits for charities. Untermyer entered his precious plants every year in the New York Flower Show. His usual rivals were John D. Rockefeller, and Mrs. R. Fulton Cutting, whose husband had built one of the most lavish and fashionable mansions of the age on the corner of 67th Street and Madison Avenue, and whose country estate in Tuxedo Park provided his wife with the competing blooms.

But with William Waite and later George Chisholm as Untermyer's talented gardeners-in-chief, the Greystone entries almost always came away with a slew of prizes.

There were family occasions, too. Frank Untermyer, Samuel's grandson, remembered tea parties held by his grandmother Minnie in the Rose Garden or one of the Color Gardens. A silver tea service and trays of pastries were brought from the mansion to the garden, set with metal chairs and tables. The children swam in the mosaic-decorated swimming pool and played tennis. A steamboat named the *Scud* was moored off a dock and sometimes their grandfather commuted in this sporty transportation to New York.

Political parties were a regular event at Greystone. One of the bigger events was the reception and garden party for the delegates and wives attending the Democratic National Convention in New York, in June 1924. The invitation carried detailed instructions: buses and cars were to leave Madison Square Garden for Greystone ("less than one hour's drive by motor") not later than 3 pm, and return at 6:30 pm by the westerly entrance. Tea would be served from 5–6 pm in front of the Walled Garden and also on the West Terrace and lawn of the mansion. Directions to the rock gardens, Walled Garden, open-air theater and swimming pool, the Vista, the six-terraced Color Gardens, Rose and Dahlia Gardens, terraced kitchen, and five walled gardens ("where it is expected there will be a fine display of rambler roses") were all carefully described in the invitation. Visitors were instructed then to go up the stairs through these gardens to another rock garden and back to the main driveway for tea.

Unfortunately, a rainstorm ruined this particular party and sent all the important guests fleeing for cover. Even Untermyer could not prevent this catastrophe, reported with glee by the local press, who noted, "Accompanying the deluge of rain was a gale of wind which blew in the tent walls and raised havoc with the supper of chicken salad, ices and hot coffee. Dishes were hurled to the lawn by wind as tables were overturned . . . " Untermyer lamented, "The storm has ruined everything. But we'll do the best we can."

Minnie Untermyer with one of her grandsons.

Not surprisingly, the spectacular visual impact of Greystone aroused the interest of the film industry. In 1923, Gloria Swanson appeared as a torch singer in a silent movie romance called *Zaza*, directed by Allan Dwan. Several scenes in the film of yearning and swooning took place at Greystone, with Walter Schott's fountain of dancing nymphs in front of the mansion featured prominently. A year later, a movie called *Twenty-One*, a "delightful satire on aesthetic dancing" starring Richard Barthelmess, in which the star plays the part of a satyr surrounded by nymphs, was filmed there. "Mr. Untermyer is recognized as one of the world's greatest connoisseurs of landscape gardening," film publicity notices purred, "and Greystone now is one vast garden. . . . Its statuary has been gathered from all parts of the world and its winding walks, its palms and its exquisite natural backgrounds make it one of the showplaces of America."

John Butler Yeats, the artist father of the famous poet, William Butler Yeats, lived in New York for much of his later life, hoping to find rich Americans who would commission him to paint their portraits. On one occasion, with this goal in mind, he made the trip to Yonkers to a party given by the Untermyers. While he failed to extract a painting commission from Mr. Untermyer, the visit made quite an impression, as he described it later in a letter to his daughter Lily:

> A beautiful house, not very big but with beautiful pictures and statues, all good. There was such a crowd of people—it took three coaches on a special train to carry us—that I had no chance of examining any of the works of art, but I could see that they were good. We had lovely music—Chopin—after the music poets and poetesses (of the latter, one a lovely girl) read their pieces.

Yeats told Lily he decided to ignore the long line of limousines that awaited guests disembarking at the station and instead walked to the house through gardens that delighted him with their rarity and beauty. Upon arrival, he was greeted by Minnie Untermyer, "who received everyone with a well-bred graciousness." At the supper, he sat next to interesting people whom he discovered were musicians and friends of I. J. Paderewski, the hugely popular pianist, composer, and prime minister of Poland in 1919.

The most intriguing moment of Yeats's visit was during a stroll through the grounds after supper, where he met a girl with "kind, sympathetic and very intelligent eyes, not at all good looking and the most ungraceful walker possible." After a pleasant talk with her, Yeats discovered that this

Dancers, including Isadora Duncan, performed often at Untermyer Gardens.

ungainly person was a professional dancer and had won an important prize in Paris for her dancing. Who could this have been? Only one young woman could possibly fit Yeats's description. This "ungraceful walker" was undoubtedly Isadora Duncan.

Another distinguished group who visited Greystone were Franz Schumann and his wife Elisabeth, who, along with composer Richard Strauss, visited the garden in September 1921. These were international artists at the height of their fame—a major coup for Minnie. Mrs. Schumann, writing in her diary, described it as "the most beautiful country estate I've ever seen. A garden with little Greek temples, an open-air theater and wonderful Greek archaeological finds. '[Max] Reinhardt must put on *A Midsummer Night's Dream* here when he comes next year,' said

Strauss." Mrs. Schumann had evidently heard a lot about Untermyer's reputation as an advocate. "Once someone paid him $300,000 not to take part in a trial!" she told her diary in amazement.

That afternoon at Greystone, Elisabeth Schumann sang some new Strauss songs, to great acclaim. The German musical celebrities were driven back to New York at about 5:30 pm, laden with boxes of flowers from the greenhouse. "Tomorrow Mrs. Untermyer is moving to her apartment in town, which is also on 5th Avenue, quite near to our hotel—and we are invited again for a meal for the day after tomorrow." She also added, with typical European thrift, "If it goes on like this we'll save a lot of money; up to now I haven't paid for a single lunch."

Articles on Greystone dominated the magazines as stories of its beauty proliferated. *Better Homes and Gardens, Nature Magazine, Country Life, American Homes of Today, Architectural Record*, and local and national newspapers all sent reporters to describe this idyllic landscape everyone was talking about. The most important garden photographers of the day, such as Mattie Edwards Hewitt, traveled to Greystone to record it for posterity. Sadly, color photography had not yet been introduced, but nobody was complaining; the sculptural and architectural features of the garden looked just fine in black and white. Untermyer's creation became a topic of conversation up and down the East Coast, and once he started opening his gardens on Tuesdays, Yonkers became a fashionable destination, whether you were a garden lover or had never looked at a flower in your life.

On a single day in October 1939, 30,000 people made their way to Greystone to see what Untermyer had wrought. Not even his greatest rivals in the garden stakes could match that figure. In a report of this invasion by the *New York Times*, George Chisholm was quoted as saying that many of the visitors came from foreign lands and distant parts of the country as well as from the city and its environs, all to see millions of chrysanthemums and pansies growing out of doors. "Additional policemen were necessary to facilitate the movement of traffic of the Albany Post Road and the movement of sightseers in and around the garden," the story

The original Temple of Love was a rectangular structure that became a popular destination for Greystone guests.

added. And, as so often was the case, Samuel Untermyer himself was to be seen mingling with the crowds, accompanied by one of his children, delighting in the admiring comments he overheard.

Untermyer's Second Act

Samuel Untermyer's new public image was not lost on anyone, least of all his enemies. It was increasingly commented on by the tabloids and analyzed cautiously by pundits. They had witnessed for years the ferocious litigator, ruthless in interrogation and tireless in debate, showing up each day wearing a small, whitish pink orchid, always fresh and very faintly scented, in his buttonhole. A replacement flower was sometimes spotted

Untermyer often enjoyed retreating to his gardens, including the Walled Garden, pictured here in its early years.

by observers, carried into the courtroom in a box like a precious jewel, then carefully unwrapped from its dampened paper and exchanged for the drooping original. (This was known to happen several times a day.) Even Walter Winchell, the most ubiquitous gossip columnist of the day, remarked on this phenomenon that had been such an intriguing part of Untermyer's courtroom appearances for so long.

By the mid-1920s, that orchid had begun to make a lot of sense. Everyone was reading about Untermyer, not in his usual confrontational role at the bar, but strolling the grounds of his lovely gardens, smiling at his guests and admiring the 3000 orchids in his greenhouse. Could it really be that this legendary giant-killer wanted only to be like Ferdinand the Bull in the children's story? Ferdinand was born and bred to be strong and fierce, trained like all young bulls to fight to the death in huge public arenas, yet all Ferdinand really wanted to do was to sit in the shade of his favorite cork tree and smell the flowers. Several commentators during these years of the garden's success noted the paradox inherent in Untermyer's career—the aggressive power broker, the "brilliant, slashing" advocate—retreating from the New York stage and instead sitting down in the shade of his favorite tree, surrounded by the flowers, scented shrubs, and bubbling fountains that he had created in his earthly Eden.

This was the man who, when asked if he aspired to political fame, had replied, "I think I might like to be parks commissioner." As Greystone took up more and more of his time, this softer side of Untermyer began to establish itself more clearly. Journalists started to recognize surprising nuances in his famously prickly character. Henry Pringle described how the lawyer would invite newspapermen to his estate on weekends. "Occasionally, to some of those who had known him the longest, he revealed himself as a man of sentiment and feeling, who, if he was a tyrant in his office and a berserker in court, loved in his home his flowers and trees and narrow paths cushioned with fragrant pine needles."

Such sentiment and feeling also revealed itself in certain acts of kindness not hitherto customary from Mr. Untermyer. He and Minnie began to share the fruits of their floriferous investment, and many people found themselves the beneficiaries of their generosity. Jean Starr Untermyer, wife of the poet Louis Untermyer, visited Greystone several times as a member of the Poetry Society, and the two couples became acquaintances in New York. At Christmas, Samuel and Minnie would deliver to the Untermyers, fresh from their greenhouses, a glowing poinsettia plant along with a large box of specially poured chocolates for their son. "Spring was sure to be announced by a box of nectarines, grown under glass on espaliered trees, each precious fruit wrapped in its square of cotton," Jean Untermeyer recalled. "In autumn I was forced to go begging to a nearby florist for a vase tall enough to hold prize chrysanthemums,

Henry Pringle said of Untermyer that he "loved in his home his flowers and trees and narrow paths cushioned with fragrant pine needles."

every lion-headed bloom as big as a salad plate, with great stems a yard and more long. At frequent intervals came a pair of tickets for a special concert which otherwise we might have missed."

In a two-part profile of Samuel Untermyer in the *New Yorker* published in 1930, the prominent journalist and muckraker Alva Johnston paid tribute to his public-spirited and generous subject by saying, "The city has not officially acknowledged its debt to its great patron even to the extent of naming a fireboat or a park after him," adding presciently, "Municipalities are ungrateful."

On Untermyer's 70th birthday in 1928, Adolph S. Ochs offered his friend a memorable tribute:

> Your life and history have been chapter after chapter of great achievements, and the rich reward of an earnest and superbly directed combination of intellect, courage, industry and high aspirations. Your world-wide fame as counselor, advocate, crusader and publicist is not an accident, or the outcome of fortuitous circumstances, but is the result of close application, self-sacrifice, a broad understanding of men and affairs, and a genuine sympathy with the great mass of struggling humanity. You have put the fear of the law in the malefactors of great wealth who had no fear of God, regardless of their fulminations, ridicule, threats, derision and scorn. Thus you have admirably served the public, and have made this service secure by drafting or inspiring much of the legislation that safeguards our institutions and provided social justice.

This was a rousing encomium. Untermyer must have been very pleased, although perhaps with one reservation. Ochs did not mention the gardens at Greystone. But then, many of his peers did not take Untermyer's most lasting achievement very seriously. For the social set, having an important garden was de rigueur, of course, as long as you bought your plants from international plant specialists and hired some well-known

A dancer performs in the waterfalls beneath the Temple of Love.

landscape architect to place them in the ground for you. Your guests could admire the design of the garden and perhaps murmur how it reminded them of Versailles. Not many "malefactors of great wealth," as Ochs called them, would have gone in for Untermyer's hands-on style of gardening. Yet the results he achieved gave him profound personal satisfaction and deeply affected all who saw these unique pleasure gardens.

Perhaps Jean Starr Untermeyer described the experience of Greystone as well as anyone:

One of the charming distractions that came about the end of the First World War was the annual entertainment offered to the Poetry Society by Mr. and Mrs. Samuel Untermyer. I believe these fetes took place early in June when flowers are at their best, for a tour of the famous Untermyer Gardens was one of the high points of the afternoon. They had a rare beauty. Visitors entered on the high plateau, where the largest garden of all—called the Greek [Walled] Garden—overlooked all the others. From there one descended by a series of narrow steps into smaller enclosures, each one planted with flowers of another color—blues, yellows, lilacs, whites, pinks—a rainbow of gardens. Far off to the side, vegetables grew in terraced rows, but well hidden behind climbing roses. There were greenhouses, in addition to the gardens, filled with exotic plants, but mostly with the celebrated Untermyer orchids.

A small stage had been erected on a grassy stretch outside the gardens, and singers and orchestra performed to an audience relaxed and comfortable under the shade of large trees. . . . Another time the Isadora Duncan girls danced for our entertainment . . . What a lovely sight they were in their flying chiffon chitons, as multi-hued as the flowers. . . . Toward evening we were bidden to tables on the wide balconies at the rear of the house, facing the Hudson River, where a delicious al fresco supper was served by such a large staff of waiters that I assumed some of them, at least, to be hired for the occasion. Then, in sighing repletion, we entered the waiting taxis and were brought to the railway station for the brief return to New York.

Ah, those were the days.

The
DECLINE

"Although I say so myself,
there is nothing in this country like it,
and it is so recognized
by all flower lovers."

—SAMUEL UNTERMYER, LETTER TO ROBERT MOSES,
AUGUST 19, 1939

The View from Yonkers

On October 7, 1939, a strange thing happened at Greystone. Paul Manship's much-admired statue of Actaeon that graced the amphitheater disappeared. Cast in bronze, it was nearly five feet tall and weighed 250 pounds. No ordinary thief could have possibly lifted this weighty object and escaped with it. The loss was discovered by Untermyer's son Irwin, who was walking in the grounds that evening. The groundskeepers immediately removed Actaeon's partner, Diana, from the amphitheater to preclude any more abductions of the garden's most famous sculptures.

Samuel Untermyer was understandably upset, expecting some enormous ransom request for the statue, which was valued at nearly $8500. (To understand the statue's value today, in 2016 the artwork's companion, Diana, was sold at auction for $727,500.) The ransom request never came, but the story made headlines locally when Untermyer offered a reward for information leading to its recovery. Two weeks after the theft, the statue turned up in a shallow hole on the premises of one John Almeider Real, a scrap metal and refuse collector. Real, after cutting up the bronze into four pieces (for easier removal, presumably), had sold the remains to an unnamed dealer for the paltry sum of $17.50. (Untermyer was furious at the low value put on his prized artwork.) But the dealer grew nervous after seeing the enormous publicity about the statue's disappearance, and never took possession of it. The pieces were then reburied in their muddy grave. Fortunately, skilled bronze workers soldered the statue together again, and it was returned, with little to show for its violent adventure, to its place in Untermyer's garden.

In 1939, the bronze statue of Actaeon in the amphitheater was stolen, cut up, and sold as scrap for $17.50. After the pieces were recovered, bronze workers were able to solder the statue back together.

The episode ended well enough, but it was odd, nonetheless. The garden suddenly seemed a little vulnerable. Was there no security? Could it have been an omen of what was to come?

At one time Samuel Untermyer was the largest single taxpayer in Yonkers. And that's saying something, for Yonkers during the period of Greystone's heyday was a gold mine of millionaires' estates lording over the banks of the Hudson River. Early photographs and paintings show ornate Victorian, Colonial, French, and Italianate villas owned by rich businessmen who liked the view and could make the commute from New York City in well under an hour. Once known as "the Queen City of the Hudson," Yonkers was home to inventors, manufacturers, and all the industrial businesses that benefited from the river and close proximity to New York for their success. In 1894, the *New York Times* described Yonkers as a city of "intelligence, culture and wealth . . . one of the most picturesque localities in Westchester County."

Sadly, this was not the same Yonkers by the time of Untermyer's death. During the late 1930s, unable to recover from the Great Depression, Yonkers experienced increasing unemployment and middle-class flight, a struggling city now treated with a certain jokey affection in the media. *The Merchant of Yonkers*, a play by Thornton Wilder, first performed in 1938, was about a rich shopkeeper living in Yonkers and looking for love. The work later evolved into *Hello Dolly*. Yonkers was again put on the map when Neil Simon wrote *Lost in Yonkers*, his play about two unhappy young boys sitting out their adolescence. By the mid-twentieth century, Yonkers itself became lost—suffering a fall from prosperity that neither Untermyer nor Bosworth, his architect, could ever have imagined.

Greystone, Anyone?

It was during this period of economic difficulty that Samuel Untermyer, now afflicted by old age, had to confront the issue of the disposition of his legendary Yonkers estate. He had first offered it to his three children, the obvious heirs, in the form of a trust. He had hoped, he said, that Greystone would be maintained and that they would establish homes of their own on the property. "Neither of these events," he later wrote grimly, "has come to pass." How badly he had misread their feelings about Greystone. It turned out that not one of them was interested, then or ever, in taking on the responsibility of their father's great garden. *New Yorker* writer Geoffrey Hellman offered a reasonable explanation for this: "Mr. Untermyer's sons, Alvin Untermyer and Judge Irwin Untermyer, have not inherited their father's costly passion for home-grown orchid boutonnieres, hothouse figs, nectarines, etc."

Samuel's son Irwin (left) became a successful judge, but he had no interest in assuming his father's legacy of Greystone and its high-maintenance gardens.

It wasn't a question of the cost, however. For starters, if they had shown any enthusiasm, the children could surely have persuaded their father to provide an endowment, while contributing some of their own considerable inheritances to the upkeep of the park. (A family member valued their legacies, placed in a joint trust, at something over $12 million, around $216 million in today's money.) But in a scenario like something out of Shakespeare, the children turned their backs on a father who, after failing them most of their lives, now begged them in vain to save his legacy.

The rebuff of their father's "costly passion for home-grown orchid boutonnieres" reflected a more complicated motive than money. It indicated all too clearly the profound ambivalence with which Alvin, Irwin, and Irene regarded their father, and, by implication, his extraordinary creation. No doubt, the sons in particular suffered from growing up in the shadow of this famous and famously autocratic public figure. Irene was closest to her father, but she became a Christian like her mother and lived elsewhere. Alvin, the oldest, also became a Christian. He married twice but had no children, and his days were spent mostly in pleasurable pursuits, with horses, polo, and an agreeable country life. His father once wrote to him complaining about the dilatory trajectory of his career. "I should hate to feel that my sons are to be parasites upon the community, living upon the efforts of those that went before them." Stern words indeed.

Irwin, the second son, married and became a respected lawyer, but created few headlines. His major claim to fame was acquiring an important collection of eighteenth- and nineteenth-century decorative arts and becoming one of the earliest Jewish trustees of the Metropolitan Museum in New York (where most of his collection ended up). Irwin's family recalls a character not dissimilar to his father's, projecting a remote and chilly manner that made him hard to love. Tragically, Irwin's wife, daughter, and two grandsons all committed suicide.

In happier times, Untermyer's granddaughter Joan and her friend Marian Sulzberger (later Heiskell), used to play at Greystone, riding their bicycles up and down the hilly paths along the river. Today, Mrs. Heiskell doesn't remember the gardens, but she remembers the enormous bank of orchids in the hall that greeted visitors to Greystone. When she arrived, she would always dutifully go upstairs with Joan to kiss the pajama-clad Mr. Untermyer ("and his whiskers") in his huge four-poster bed. "And when we ate a meal in the dining room, there were always place cards!" Another young family member, Louise Untermyer Frankel, remembers visits to Greystone "where the butler, Blair, would give us each a cookie and an orchid."

One need not be a psychiatrist to understand why the patriarch could not find any of his children willing to inherit Greystone. Samuel Untermyer was a demanding, distant father who did not give his children the confidence they desperately needed. If there was love or attention, it seemed directed toward the garden rather than to them. So powerful was this

Samuel Untermyer's granddaughter Joan and her friend Marian
riding bicycles at Greystone in 1930.

pervading chill that it spilled over to the next generation. Irwin's son Frank was openly hostile regarding Greystone, saying "We hated the place," and expressing his wish not to be buried in the family plot at Woodlawn.

Shortly after Samuel Untermyer died, publisher Alfred Knopf asked Geoffrey Hellman, whose profile of Untermyer in the *New Yorker* had been very well received, if he'd write Untermyer's biography. When Hellman requested Alvin Untermyer's permission for the project, Alvin responded that after discussion with his siblings, they had decided to turn Hellman down. Why? Were they afraid of some dark secret in the family? The out-of-wedlock baby who died in infancy? Alvin's own illegitimate birth? There were also rumors of sharp practice in Samuel's early career. Or might it have been that after a lifetime of intimidation and distance, perhaps the children were finally taking a small but significant revenge?

The Question of an Endowment

If Samuel Untermyer suffered from his children's damning rejection of his beloved Greystone, there is no record of it. But by 1939, he was increasingly aware of the limits of his own mortality, and the future of Greystone became a matter of extreme urgency. In the late summer of 1939, he began a three-pronged appeal to the local institutions he thought might take over the property. On August 1 of that year he offered Greystone to the City of Yonkers. His statement, printed in the local newspapers, included the plea that "I want to do something for the city in which I have lived for so many years. . . . If the City of Yonkers will maintain the estate in its dignified and beautiful fashion, I will be glad to give the city my parks and gardens."

Once it was announced that Samuel Untermyer was offering his house and estate to the city, he received a torrent of letters, commending his generosity and making suggestions for the property—an old people's home, perhaps, or a yeshiva trade school. One correspondent asked if he could come over and take cuttings from the garden. But most of the letter writers asked him for money—sad, begging letters, describing their plight and hoping for a handout from this impossibly rich man who could actually afford to give away a mansion and over a hundred acres of land. "I'm just a poor old lady," one writer pleaded. It was a painful response to his misguided act of generosity.

When the City of Yonkers refrained from immediately responding to Untermyer's offer, he saw he must try other avenues, and turned to Robert Moses, perhaps the most influential parks commissioner New York City ever had. On August 19, 1939, Untermyer wrote to Moses, inviting him to visit Greystone and see for himself what a wonderful place it was. "The grounds of Greystone include a vast amount of statuary and antique foreign gates gathered during the years past by Mrs. Untermyer and myself in our many visits to European countries," he boasted. "Greystone's collection of foreign rhododendrons has been valued at $250,000."

Untermyer approached New York City parks commissioner Robert Moses about the Greystone estate, but Moses wanted an endowment, which Untermyer said he could not provide.

He pointed out that Mrs. Russell Sage, another rhododendron collector, had presented the City of New York with 10,000 small rhododendron plants which were planted in Central Park, "all of which have disappeared as the result of ignorance and criminal neglect—whilst mine have grown into large and sturdy plants."

This was surely not the best way to approach Robert Moses. Known as the "czar of the city," Moses was promoting a huge program of new buildings and highways that was transforming the urban landscape. More to the point, Moses was an outspoken populist, disparaging such offenders as the old-money "snooty" trustees of the Metropolitan Museum of Art, with whom he battled incessantly over their development plans. No wonder Untermyer's enthusiastic descriptions of his "antique foreign gates" and his "foreign rhododendrons" didn't go over so well with this particular chairman of New York's parks.

Moses responded to Untermyer's letter by saying he saw no reason to visit Greystone until a very important condition was established: the promise of an endowment of "at least $1 million." (Over $17 million in today's money.) Untermyer was shocked. "I am greatly discouraged," he wrote. "I had, in fact, intended to endow it, but conditions have so radically changed that I am not in a position to contribute to an endowment." Deadlock. Moses set down his decision as follows: "Greystone should, if possible, be accepted as a public park. It would be a city park, not only because it is within the city limits, but because as Yonkers grows this estate will be needed primarily for local park purposes. Greystone does not fit the definition of either a county or a state park." Moses went on to say that it was clear to him that without an endowment, neither the county nor the state would accept the gift.

Once again Untermyer found himself involved in a trial, but this time it was to save a garden, not a client. In desperation, he turned to Herbert Lehman, the governor of New York. "I cannot put in funds with which to endow it," he explained to the Governor, "as that would cost a million dollars. There was a time when I was not only willing but anxious to do this, but the enormous income taxes and the reduction in the value of securities generally would render it unjust to my family. They simply could not afford it."

Untermyer then again put forward his case for Greystone. "Greystone has cost me, in one way or another, in the neighborhood of $500,000 [nearly $9 million today]. I spent a million and a half in the construction of the Greek Garden alone; and the place is filled with rare trees, shrubs and thousands of rhododendrons, which render it unique. I wish you could come around with Mrs. Lehman sometime this month and look at it. . . . There is nothing in the country like it." He then added, "Mrs.

It was heartbreaking for Untermyer to learn that no local or state agency was interested in his gift of Greystone and its magnificent gardens.

Untermyer and I gathered the statuary in the park for the past forty or fifty years, unto the time of her death, from all over the world."

How naive was he? The year he was trying to unload Greystone was 1939, in a country barely emerging from a traumatic economic depression. Moreover, the United States was looking at a European political crisis that soon turned into the Second World War. This was no time to be distracted by allocating sums of money for increasingly irrelevant projects like a rich man's garden. Untermyer's timing was abysmal, and, unusually for him, the tone of his argument to Moses and Lehman was all wrong. His son Alvin picked up on the inappropriate message he read in his father's letters. "It makes it look as though you are more concerned about perpetuating, at public expense, the maintenance of your particular abode and something that you built up, rather than providing an appropriate park for the underprivileged public."

The Yonkers City Planning Board originally saw the steep slopes and rocky terrain that characterized parts of the Untermyer estate as a detriment to its use as a park.

Untermyer's last hope, the Yonkers City Planning Board, also failed him. The board members opined that the expenses of maintaining the park in the way it should be maintained were unforthcoming. They also pointed out that the park was not conducive to the public interest, in that its steep and rocky slopes would not be amenable to recreational use such as ball fields. Another objection was that Yonkers already had a perfectly acceptable public park by the river, Trevor Park. Why take on the burden of another? But the most pressing reason for its rejection was the loss of taxes, amounting to $34,000 each year, if Greystone were taken over by the Westchester County Park Commission.

Untermyer had run out of options. After these painful exchanges with the authorities in Yonkers and New York, there was nowhere else to turn. Increasingly weak and struggling for breath in his Palm Springs retreat, he was further undermined by what was clearly a humiliating public repudiation of his proudest achievement. Just over six months after his pleading letter to Herbert Lehman, Samuel Untermyer was dead.

Paradise Lost

But Untermyer had the last laugh, even if a hollow one. After his death on March 17, 1940, his will revealed that he had left the Greystone estate in turn to the three institutions that had rejected him: first to New York State, to be designated with the name "Samuel Untermyer Park and Gardens." If New York State did not accept the conditions within six months, then the offer would go to Westchester County. If this offer was also rejected, the City of Yonkers, lucky loser, would get the gift. The results were not unexpected. After the legal procedures were completed, Greystone, like an unwanted child, was turned down by all three candidates. Perhaps the biggest surprise to everyone involved, however, was that according to the will, Samuel Untermyer's net estate, not including the family trust, was worth roughly $9 million (roughly $158 million in today's money),

Hundreds of treasures from the Untermyer estate were sold and auctioned off after Samuel's death. This British porcelain set remained with his son Irwin, however, and was gifted to the Metropolitan Museum of Art.

mostly in stocks and bonds, and not including his real estate. Could he really not have afforded an endowment?

In May 1940, Parke-Bernet gallery ran a two-day auction at Greystone of the late Samuel Untermyer's possessions. Some of the more important items had already been sold privately. Geoffrey Hellman, doing research for his profile on Untermyer, visited Greystone that spring when the place was being stripped of its treasures in preparation for the sale. He observed the contents with dubious enthusiasm: "odd clocks, tapestries, jade bowls, polar-bear rugs, brown grizzly-bear rugs, black-bear rugs, Bengal-tiger rugs, embroidered cushions, punch bowls, statuettes, screens, chandeliers, and gas lighting fixtures." Large amounts of Chinese porcelain, carvings, and lacquer, English china, silver services, glassware, and candlesticks covered every table and sideboard, tagged with numbers. Hundreds of books were piled up in the library (mainly law and detective stories, Untermyer's favorites), along with busts of Sophocles, Solon, and Untermyer himself.

Neptune gazes forlornly over Samuel Untermyer's rapidly declining property.
The statue later disappeared and was never recovered.

But when it came to asset-stripping, it was the garden furniture on offer that revealed the extent of Untermyer's reach. The collection was spectacular: stone urns, carved lions, Greek and Roman marbles, dancing nymphs and goddesses, Georgian statuettes, a six-foot-high fountain surmounted by a bronze figure of Neptune, an Italian Renaissance stone wellhead, and a gorgeous, late-Gothic, sculptured limestone oval jardinière. Reading these lists today, one gets a vivid impression of how splendid the garden must have looked with these ornaments everywhere. Some of them went for very high prices, even in those difficult economic times.

As for the thousands of precious orchids and rare plants, these were auctioned off separately on the second day. The Vegetable Gardens remained relatively untouched, but 4000 chickens had already been sold from the poultry pens, and the flowers, shrubs, and hundreds of fruits from the greenhouses all went under the auctioneer's hammer.

After the sales, settlement of Untermyer's will began to move slowly through the courts. In an ironic twist, his children were drawn in to play an active role in the disposition of their father's property, finding it necessary to set up a nonprofit trust to manage the park and gardens.

Meanwhile, the City of Yonkers was having second thoughts, and after commissioning a survey of the land in 1943, it decided to accept seventy acres of the property from the family trust. Sixteen acres were designated "Samuel Untermyer Park and Gardens." This became part of the land that makes up the gardens today. In a decision handed down by the Court of Appeals, the rest of the one hundred fifty acres would be sold off.

But delays continued. In 1948, Yonkers decided to obtain another survey of the property. H. Armour Smith, a member of the city's planning department, made a detailed inventory and found much to his liking, including the boxwood collection (which, he remarked, represented "a lot of money"), the statuary in the Walled Garden, the waterworks, the Color Gardens with their marble dolphin fountains, and the vistas. "There is much of value running wild or going to ruin on the property," he concluded, and declared that "this magnificent property is a rare combination of natural beauties and high development. Certainly, the many superb vistas cannot be surpassed within the range of the Palisades. The City now has the opportunity to create the most outstanding and highly developed Park on the Hudson River, embracing a beautiful wild-life sanctuary . . . The possibilities are immense." What vindication for Untermyer!

Yonkers, however, was unimpressed with Mr. Smith's enthusiastic evaluation. The city sold 24 of its remaining 70 acres to a developer. The mansion was razed, leaving a large hole. Permission for construction of a cardiac hospital (later a residence) was granted. Garden apartments

The Vista and its overlook, once the highlight of the visitor's tour,
was reduced to a series of broken steps and overrun by weeds.

were built across the street in 1953. Finally, in 1962, the parcel of land north of the Walled Garden was sold to St. John's Riverside Hospital for $20,000. The hospital proceeded to expand, building a multistory pavilion and an array of parking lots sloping down toward the river, much of this development swallowing up what had once been the Vegetable Gardens and part of the Rose and Color Gardens.

Within a little over 20 years, Samuel Untermyer's garden had shrunk to a sliver, its radiant arbors and borders now enclosed by apartment buildings, two hospitals, and parking lots. The glamorous statues, columns, temple structures, and staircases so carefully designed by Welles Bosworth were sold, broken, disintegrating or stolen. Only one sculpture was extracted from the estate—Walter Schott's fountain with the dancing nymphs. This lovely piece, star of the movies, was given in 1947 by the Untermyer family to New York's Conservatory Garden in Central Park, where it still stands. The flowers, shrubs, and trees, so lavishly planted by Waite, Chisholm, and their teams, disappeared, died, or became engulfed in invasive vines and weeds. The lawns and pathways were smothered in brambles and uncontrolled vegetation. The waterfalls and fountains had

The Rose and Dahlia Gardens, unrecognizable
after years of neglect and abandonment.

dried up. The swimming pool was filled with dirt for safety, totally bury-
ing the delicate mosaics. As a powerful reminder of the garden's glorious
history, the core structure of the Walled Garden and amphitheater still
stood bravely in place, as well as the Carriage House outside the garden
walls, where once had been greenhouses.

This was the garden's darkest hour. People no longer strolled along
its paths, smelling the flowers and admiring the view. Residents no longer wanted to bring their children to what had become a scary jungle
of junkyard clutter and overgrown weeds. The people it attracted now
were the homeless and kids who wanted to get drunk or high. The 1960s
saw new groups of hippies appreciating its mysterious, echoing spaces.
Musicians could come and play as loudly as they liked. "The amphitheater
was available for love feasting through a shrubbery hole. Great place for
guitar," said one visitor from the period. The park became a perfect place
for such activities, since it was not policed and indifferently maintained
by the city. After dark, the graffiti-covered walls, fragments of crumbling
statuary, and shapeless shrubs created a theater of menace, encouraging
drug users and petty criminals to congregate.

Greystone: A Horror Movie

In the early 1970s, emergency plans were formed to stop the increasing desecration and dangers to be found in Untermyer's garden. It was by this time an eyesore for all residents of Yonkers. Funds for the program of restoration were raised from an urban beautification grant and the City of Yonkers. A local architect named James Piccone was hired to make a plan to restore some of the prime architecture of the garden, in particular the Walled Garden and the Vista. Much of the work consisted of repairing or replacing the limestone walls of the Walled Garden as well as structural cleaning and patching of the octagonal towers and terraces. The turrets, once open to the public, had been closed for years to deter those climbing up to seek Nirvana.

According to Mr. Piccone, "We spent a year patching, repointing, supporting weak walls temporarily, and so on, to stabilize badly deteriorated but salvageable sections of the park before we were able to proceed with full-fledged construction." Work also started on Bosworth's beloved mosaics in the amphitheater. The dirt in the swimming pool was removed and replaced with water, revealing the damaged floor. The steps of the Vista were relaid and trees replanted along the stone walls leading down to the river.

In 1975, John Lennon was photographed beneath the Temple of Love, giving much-needed positive publicity to the garden. The famous Beatle had prompted this by saying to his friend, photographer Bob Gruen, "Let's go into nature. The sun is shining and I bought a new suit, so we can take a few summer pictures." Bob Gruen suggested going to Untermyer Park. Apparently, his girlfriend remembered it from high school and had told him how beautiful it was. So they went to the park and took pictures. However, an indication that the garden wasn't entirely in the pristine state of its gloried past was a revealing remark made by Lennon during their walk through the park, according to a German journalist who was also present. "Bob," said John, "this is really wonderful to go through all these bushes. I should have worn jeans: now I'm totally messed up!"

John Lennon posed in the Temple of Love in 1975. The delicate dome remained intact despite the sad state of affairs in other parts of the gardens.

But even a visit from John Lennon could not work the required magic. In 1976, work on the garden came to an abrupt halt when a financial crisis hit the city and all funding dried up. Any further repair and replacement as recommended by Piccone was canceled, including his plan to convert the Carriage House into a visitors' center, which was twice burned down by arsonists during reconstruction. Yet this ill-fated program of restoration, while ending in frustration, still showed some hope of rescue and somehow kept Piccone's vision of the garden alive.

In the midst of this economic stalemate, another blow further dashed hopes for the park's revival. This time the wound was more psychic than physical. During 1976 and 1977, a serial killer roamed the streets of New York and Yonkers, murdering a seemingly random group of young women. In crazed letters sent to journalists and the police, signed "Son of Sam," the killer hinted at dreadful crimes committed in Untermyer Park against humans and dogs. The people of Yonkers were terrified; the whole country went on alert at these horrifying stories.

The cult was identified as the Process Church of Final Judgment, founded by Robert de Grimston and his wife Mary Anne. Stories spread about the cult's fanatical worship of a combination of Christ and Satan, with blood sacrifices taking place every Saturday night in an old pump house near the aqueduct at the park's western perimeter. It became a perfect place for such activities, since it was remote and unvisited by the general public. Both the pump house and gatehouse nearby were later found to have macabre graffiti on the walls.

Night-shift workers at the adjacent hospital claimed to see torch flames flickering deep within the park's heavily wooded areas. Strange chanting was also frequently heard around the pump house, which became known as the Devil's Cave. Perhaps the most distressing detail of these alleged cult ceremonies was a 1976 police report documenting the finding of dead and mutilated German shepherd dogs in the aqueduct. The local

Graffiti and derelict plants took over the pump house.

One of Bosworth's many beloved mosaics, vandalized almost beyond repair.

Yonkers newspaper, the *Herald Statesman*, picked up on this story with relish, describing cult members at meetings near the aqueduct "sacrificing dogs and drinking their blood." While the slaughter of dogs was never definitively proved to be part of the cult's activities, an interesting fact is that de Grimston's wife, who divorced him and left the cult, later founded the Best Friends Animal Society, an animal welfare organization.

The serial killer was finally identified as David Berkowitz, a resident of Yonkers. On August 10, 1977, he was arrested outside his apartment building, hardly a mile from Untermyer Park, through whose haunted pathways and woods he had so often wandered. He confessed to all the crimes. He was tried, found guilty, and given six consecutive life sentences, which he is still serving.

Berkowitz later disclaimed his connection to the cult. But the damage was done. Once again, Untermyer's garden saw sad times. Graffiti, garbage, uncontrolled weeds, downed trees, and further deterioration of the remaining statuary greeted anyone bold enough to venture into this blighted landscape.

Almost two decades later, a historic landscape report on Untermyer Park was commissioned by the City of Yonkers, through the cooperative efforts of the Department of Parks, Recreation and Conservation and the Yonkers Landmarks Preservation Board. It was produced by LAND-SCAPES, a landscape architecture, planning, and historic preservation organization based in Connecticut and Vermont. In 1995, their massive and very thorough report was published. Here is part of their summary of the state of Untermyer Park at the end of the 1970s:

> Although the setting, topography, and views and vistas were all intact, the boundaries of the property had shrunk drastically with the change of the property from a private estate to a public landscape. This functional change was also reflected in the loss of all of the estate's original buildings, including the Mansion, Carriage House, greenhouses, and support buildings and servants' residences. . . . The spatial organization of the gardens, too, changed, as the Color Gardens, Vegetable Gardens, and Rose Garden were lost to vandalism, overgrowth and lack of maintenance by new owners.

The writers explained that pedestrians could only visit the Walled Garden and the Vista, and noted, perhaps with implicit regret, that some of the repair work already completed on walls, balustrades, and paving was not made with original materials. Their conclusion was uncompromising:

> The conditions found today within Untermyer Park are dire. Deterioration is proceeding and in several cases, results in unsafe conditions.

Agreeing that the park ("a special place") deserved to be brought back into full use and enjoyment, they warned that "a concerted effort will be required."

Not an encouraging progress report. With the strange history of the cult overshadowing the already error-prone efforts to recreate that "special place" once admired and treasured by so many Americans, Samuel Untermyer's dream, like the great Gatsby's in Scott Fitzgerald's novel, seemed to "be borne back ceaselessly into the past."

Requiem for a Garden

Gone. Except for the Walled Garden, all gone. Every flower in the Color Gardens, every vegetable in the Vegetable Gardens, every exotic fruit and plant in the greenhouses, Bosworth's Italian terraces, the rocky grottoes, all gone. And the thousands of orchids—gone.

The rows of precious boxwood, now shapeless blobs. The elegant paths, pools, and pavilions marking the flower beds, vanished. The mosaics, cracked and moldy. The spectacular staircase down to the river, reduced to crumbling steps and crawling vines. The Vista, almost invisible, blocked by overgrown trees and shrubs. The noble Palisades on the other side of the river, no longer discernable.

Of the astonishing spectacle Untermyer had crafted, only 16 acres were left out of 150. From order to wilderness, in roughly 30 years.

But perhaps the most striking symptom of the distress caused by Untermyer's death was the decline of his mausoleum at Woodlawn Cemetery. It was always something of a puzzle. Paul Chalfin, who designed it, was not a professional architect. The reason Untermyer commissioned him was perhaps because Welles Bosworth, the more obvious choice, had disappeared to France with his favorite client, John D. Rockefeller Jr. Untermyer knew Chalfin through the Palm Beach social scene, and Chalfin had gained considerable acclaim for his brilliant design work at

The gatehouse, marred by graffiti and about to be claimed by greedy vines.

Vizcaya in Miami. Untermyer needed someone to get to work quickly after his wife's unexpected death.

The design Chalfin came up with was definitely unorthodox. Instead of the Parthenons, Gothic chapels, and Egyptian temples built for Untermyer's neighbors in the cemetery, Chalfin, evidently respecting the interests of his client, came up with a kind of garden. A lawn gently slopes up a hill. On one side is space for the graves of Untermyer family members, and a long series of stepped terraces on the other is laid out to accommodate others over time. At the far end of the lawn, a large semicircular stone exedra frames a piazza inlaid with a star that has a bronze fountain (originally planned as a sundial) at its center. In Chalfin's plans, the star was originally made of black pebbles, reminiscent of the pebble mosaics Bosworth used at Kykuit. Other aspects of the landscaping perhaps make reference to Greystone, such as the amphitheater and the masses of

Even the once-spectacular Untermyer mausoleum at Woodlawn Cemetery
was largely abandoned, with the 150 rhododendrons planted upon
Samuel's death lost to neglect.

rhododendrons. Some have suggested that the star is the Star of David, but it doesn't really resemble one, and none of Chalfin's extant plans refer to it as such. Moreover, the mausoleum was designed originally to memorialize Untermyer's beloved wife Minnie, who was not Jewish.

Perhaps the most unusual aspect of the design is the memorial monument itself. A long, undecorated wall, originally backed by dense plantings of rhododendrons, runs along the western perimeter of the plot. It stops short just before it meets a rectangular shrine rising up from a stone plinth, with heavy carved bronze doors on three sides. Four columns, framing the doors, support a bronze stepped roof in Hindu style. The shrine sits on a rusticated stone base, accessed by steps leading up from

The tomb's bronze doors and sculpture, by Gertrude Vanderbilt Whitney, were destined to survive. Without regular maintenance, however, the surrounding plantings could not.

the side of the plot (presumably the original entry to the mausoleum) to a platform where one can sit on a curved stone bench and admire the monument in its entirety.

Chalfin asked his friend Gertrude Vanderbilt Whitney to design the bronze doors and their interior, and she agreed, for the huge fee of $65,000 (over $900,000 in today's value). At the time of this assignment, she was busy with one of her most important commissions, a memorial to the American Expeditionary Force in St. Nazaire, France. Her work for this war memorial was compelling: a soldier stands on an eagle at the top of a stone column rising out of the waters of St. Nazaire harbor. As she worked on this sculpture, perhaps the tragic images of war carried over in her imagination to the Untermyer work, for she created three ghostly, grieving figures enclosed in the elaborately sculpted bronze doors. The doors bear Greek inscriptions: on the left door, "motherhood" and "charity"; on the center door, "nurturing, service, inspiration"; and on the right door, "friendship and brotherhood."

Chalfin didn't know at first what his friend was planning. His early sketches for the monument showed two figures on top of a plinth decorated with wreaths, a far more conventional memorial. Indeed, Whitney's design produced some tension between Chalfin and Untermyer. A 1925 note indicates that Untermyer wanted a "radically different treatment" of the monument—for instance, looking for a small "edifice" as a base rather than a pedestal. What he made of the conical stepped roof and the carved bronze doors is not recorded. Did he see the whole structure as an homage to the Indian and Greek themes of Bosworth's walled garden at Greystone? Was he happy with Chalfin's final design for the shrine? We don't know. The whole thing had to be built in a hurry, for Minnie's death came as a surprise, and nobody wanted to make her wait in her bronze casket outside the mausoleum while delays in construction postponed installation.

Samuel Untermyer left a permanent endowment for the mausoleum in his will, and Whitney's heavy bronze work used in the monument ensured its longevity. But after Untermyer's death, the rest of the plot soon began to disintegrate. The magnificent plantings of rhododendrons, azaleas, kalmias, and ivy were lost. The boxwood became overgrown. Trees died. The masonry began to decay. The waterworks dried up. Shrouded in tangled weed trees, looming darkly at the top of its little mountain, the mausoleum, like Greystone, was coming undone. Chisholm loyally tended to the place as best he could until around 1946, when it was clear that the endowment for its upkeep would not be nearly enough. Frantic estimates were mailed by the Woodlawn landscapers to Untermyer's children over the years, with only marginal success.

The writer V. S. Naipaul once used the expression, "The debris of a life." He could have been describing the wasteland that was once Untermyer's garden. Perhaps the saddest sight was discovered by a visitor stumbling through the ruins of Greystone's carriage house in the 1940s. Scattered on the floor was a heap of faded blue ribbons, abandoned relics of Untermyer's award-winning rhododendrons. "Debris," Naipaul went on to write, "which nonetheless never ceased to have an element of grandeur." It was this debris at Untermyer Park, with its elements of grandeur, that inspired its rescue.

The
RESCUE

"The Untermyer estate is
a one-in-a-million property."

—STEPHEN F. BYRNS, 1995

The Planting of a Seed

Stephen Byrns was born in 1954 in a small town in Michigan. As a child, he liked building things—tree houses, castles, igloos. The soil at his house was sandy and the grass always looked dry and brown. "So I got a hose and sprayed it with water," he remembers, "and it turned green!" This magical transformation started his interest in growing things, no matter where the seeds came from. "Wonder Bread had a seed packet attached to the loaf, and I planted the seeds," he recalls. "They grew into marigolds!" By the time he was 16, his family had moved to his great-aunt's house on Lake Michigan, where there had once been a sizable garden. Steve spent many summers restoring it. The seeds had been planted, so to speak, early and well.

After studying history and architecture at Princeton, he decided to focus solely on architecture as a graduate student. With a master's degree from Columbia, in 1985 Byrns became a founder of BKSK Architects, in New York. For the next 30 years, he worked on residential buildings, developments, commercial projects, and new buildings in Brooklyn, Tribeca, and Riverdale. He became involved with historic preservation and learned about the neighborhoods surrounding New York City, some of which still retained their traditions of parks and open space.

But living in Manhattan ceased to please him. He hadn't forgotten his childhood love of gardens. In 1988, he moved with his partner, artist and teacher Thomas Lollar, to Yonkers. In Yonkers, they found an eight-bedroom house overlooking the river that was wonderful, if far too

Architect Stephen Byrns (right) and Timothy Tilghman, head gardener at the Untermyer Gardens Conservancy. Byrns championed the restoration of the gardens and now serves as the Conservancy's president.

big for their needs. The move was a catalyst of sorts for Byrns. Inspired by a community of artists, writers, and pioneers of various kinds that Steve found in Yonkers, he became very involved in local issues of preservation. He joined clubs and started house tours, and learned the challenges of civic activism, "to help preserve where we lived."

During this period, he discovered Untermyer Park, which had become badly decayed. He began to learn its history, gave some tours there, and became intrigued by its former glory. Meanwhile, the valuable land that still belonged to the park was under continual threat. Steve became involved in a campaign to prevent the Vegetable Gardens from being destroyed for a nursing home. He pleaded with everyone, from the president of the hospital to the Yonkers City Council. He wrote articles and

The gardens waited patiently while sales and details of property ownership were negotiated.

letters. No luck. During his exploration of the proposed development land, he found remnants of the cobalt-blue tiles that had once been part of Bosworth's water channels. Steve had become an archeologist, and the site of Untermyer Park became his dig. But so much now was lost. "It was like Beirut," he said. "It was too far gone."

In the 1970s, the cardiac hospital had sold a package of land for a low-rise development to be designed by the renowned architect Richard Meier. The developer of the project went bankrupt, however, and in 1986 the land was sold to another developer, who planned to build a 665-unit condominium there. The second developer also went bankrupt.

Another pair of local activists entered the lists. Nortrud Spero, a real estate agent who had worked with Byrns on finding his house in Yonkers, strongly encouraged Byrns in his fledgling efforts to restore the park. In June 1992, Joseph Koslowsky, an appraiser and supporter of the Old

A major turning point in the rescue of the gardens was when the City of Yonkers closed a deal to increase Untermyer Park from 16 to 43 acres.

Croton Aqueduct, spotted a legal notice buried in tiny print in the Yonkers *Herald Statesman* announcing the projected sale of the condominium project, now in the hands of the bankers. He knew this could be critical to the future of the park. He took it to Nortrud Spero, and the two moved quickly. Ms. Spero negotiated with the Open Space Institute (OSI) and the Trust for Public Land to save the land from its condominium fate. The OSI brokered a deal with the bank to reduce the debt, and in 1996, the city closed a deal to buy the land and return it to Untermyer Park. (Two additional acres of the land were given to the Richmond Children's Center at the southern end of the estate.) By a stroke of the pen, Untermyer Park had expanded from 16 acres to 43. ("If it had remained at 16 acres, I might not have become involved," Byrns admitted later.)

In 1997, Steve and Thomas found a more suitable home in Riverdale, with four bedrooms and one and a half gorgeous acres of land overlooking the Hudson River. The house had been owned by Ruth Rea Howell, a distinguished gardener who has a garden named after her at the New York Botanical Garden. How could Steve not be seduced by it? He promptly set to work to restore the great work of his predecessor, doubling the size of Mrs. Howell's original garden. To his delight, the house was only two blocks south of Wave Hill in the Bronx, one of the most famous public gardens on the Eastern seaboard, and a favorite of Steve's. He became a friend of Marco Polo Stufano, the garden's longtime director of horticulture, and joined the board in 2000, a position he held for 10 years. In 2004, he became a commissioner on the New York City Landmarks Preservation Commission, another move that seemed to be inexorably leading him to the derelict gardens on the riverbank in Yonkers.

The Romance of Ruins

In 2010, Steve Byrns went to a party in Yonkers, where his friend and neighbor, artist Richard Haas, mentioned that the fountains in Untermyer Park had been turned on. This was extraordinary news, Steve remembers thinking. The City of Yonkers had actually been doing some remedial work, and there were supporters, like architect Ralph Crosby, who cared enough to attempt some restoration work.

Something felt different to Byrns in 2010. The fountains seemed like a symbol of hope. "I felt like something had hit me," he said. "The place combined history, gardens, architecture, horticulture, and an important piece of America's cultural and social heritage." As he walked through the jungle of tangled weeds and crumbled stonework, he sensed the power of what lay beneath. "I am attracted to things gone to seed," he said, "the romance of ruins." The fact that the fountains managed to pour out even trickles of water was an epiphany. It proved to him that the gardens were somehow alive under all the rubble, that Untermyer's grand creation was not lost forever, that somehow the garden could be brought back to life.

Once fountains were turned back on at the gardens, Byrns felt
a sense of hope that renovation was possible.

Byrns heard the call. It was faint, at first. Resurrecting a garden is not an easy thing in the best of times. In fact, it has never been at the forefront of the American gardening agenda. Unlike in Britain, where the National Trust has been operating since the late nineteenth century to preserve historic houses and gardens, Americans tend to like making their own landscapes, each new generation to their own. Tear down the old and build the new. Only recently have people realized the importance of America's garden heritage, and turned their attention to preserving gardens as well as houses. Beatrix Farrand's last garden, for instance, Garland Farm in Bar Harbor, Maine, was rescued plant by plant, path by path, flower by flower, from almost certain oblivion. Referring to early drawings and photographs, and using archeological techniques like those used in the restoration of an ancient Egyptian tomb, the restorers painstakingly recreated and opened to the public this most precious of Farrand's creations.

Other famous rescues have entered the garden history books. The island gardens of Alcatraz in northern California, once a creative and spiritual outlet for hardened criminals under an enlightened warden's secretary, were abandoned and forgotten when the prison closed down, only to be recreated and replanted in 2003 for over a million tourists who now visit Alcatraz every year. The romantic Southern estate of Godfrey Barnsley, in Adairsville, Georgia, was decimated by war and natural disasters, until a European prince arrived in 1888 and pulled it back from the ruins, one of the few antebellum gardens surviving in the South. The delightfully personal garden of the African-American poet and civil rights activist Anne Spencer in Lynchburg, Virginia, was brought back to life by a local garden club and passionate supporters after years of neglect.

But obstacles to the rescue of Untermyer Park appeared from many quarters. Representatives of the City of Yonkers did not share Byrns's enthusiasm. It was not an ideal site for a public park, everyone knew that. Local residents were equally uninspired. Who could possibly find the money to do all the work required? Who would do the work? Who would pay the gardeners?

Every corner of the estate cried for attention, and Byrns was prepared to lead the reclamation effort.

But there was no going back now. Steve renegotiated his contract with his architecture firm to work part-time, and in late 2010, he resigned from his positions at the Landmarks Preservation Commission and Wave Hill. He approached Marco Polo Stufano, who had retired from Wave Hill, about the possibility of Stufano working on the Untermyer project. Wave Hill, of course, had itself been rescued from destruction years earlier and turned into a public garden. But Byrns had no idea what a remarkable chain of connections he had inadvertently exposed.

It turned out that Stufano had been a student of T. H. Everett, the legendary horticulturist and senior staffer at the New York Botanical Garden. Everett, like Untermyer's men Waite and Chisholm, had shipped out to New York from England in the late 1920s to seek his fortune in the field of horticulture, and one of Samuel Untermyer's agents had found

While the Untermyer grounds had been designated a park,
Byrns wanted to refocus attention on the gardens.

him at the docks and recruited him to work as a gardener at Greystone. Everett didn't stay in Yonkers long. He joined the New York Botanical Garden in 1932 and remained there as a distinguished scholar and teacher until his death in 1986.

In the 1960s, Marco Polo Stufano was a student at the New York Botanical Garden. Everett recognized Stufano's talent, calling him "the best student I ever had." He took Stufano to see Untermyer Park. Walking through the forlorn remains, Everett, who had once heaped praise on Welles Bosworth's garden design, regaled his young student with stories of how magnificent the gardens had looked in their heyday. So when Steve Byrns came to Stufano in 2010, it was as though everything, as Stufano said, had come full circle. Like the blue tiles Steve had stumbled upon, here was another connection, an irresistible link, this time from Stufano's past. Stufano immediately agreed to join the crusade to restore the garden that his mentor had so vividly described to him.

One of Byrns's priorities concerned the name of the project he was undertaking. Samuel Untermyer had named his legacy "Samuel Untermyer Park and Gardens." Steve felt that the place was no longer a park, strictly speaking. Wishing to emphasize the gardens, he decided to rename his organization the Untermyer Gardens Conservancy. When Marco Polo Stufano recommended a former gardener from Wave Hill, Timothy Tilghman, to become the Conservancy's first gardener, Steve knew that he had his dream team. But he would need support both from the City of Yonkers and from the power players in New York. He had to find the money. He had to make a master plan. He had to create a board. By 2011, the huge task had begun.

The Master Plan

The work started in the Walled Garden, where some restoration had taken place earlier. Byrns wrote of the first achievements under his directorship:

> Trees, shrubs, perennials, tropicals, aquatic plants, and annuals—thousands of plants—have been planted . . . In addition, the area around the Temple of Love has been cleared of 70 years of overgrowth, exposing a substantial chain of rock gardens. The mile-long carriage trail connecting to the Old Croton Aqueduct has been cleared for the first time in a generation and is now passable. The Vista has been kept clear of weeds and two of the Color Gardens are now visible in their ruined form. Weekly public tours have been given throughout the growing season of 2012, as well as countless private tours for garden clubs and scholarly societies. Walk-in visitation as well has jumped substantially.

In the following years, the restoration expanded exponentially. One mile of eight-foot deer fence plus seasonal lighting were installed (2015). The amphitheater was restored. More work on the Walled Garden took place.

TOP LEFT Significant earth moving was necessary to update garden systems and ensure the property was on solid ground. TOP RIGHT One of the first projects tackled was the Temple of Love. A new pipe system was installed for the waterfalls. ABOVE Once seven decades of overgrowth was removed from the rock gardens beneath the Temple of Love, the rocks were restored and new plants were installed.

TOP LEFT Canals and pools in the Walled Garden were dismantled and rebuilt with modern irrigation. TOP RIGHT The unicorn at the gatehouse entrance received a new head. ABOVE Mosaic tiles that had graced the interior of the Temple of the Sky were painstakingly replaced.

The Temple of Love, after its rocks were restored
but before plants and water were added.

In 2016, Stephen Byrns resigned from his architecture firm and became
the Untermyer Garden Conservancy's first president, with a full-time sal-
ary. Fund-raising was accelerated and people responded with enthusiasm.
There were parties, articles, visitors, newsletters. A seasonal gardener was
hired. The Temple of Love, with its filigree, wrought-iron dome, and the

Waterfalls, flowers, and other plantings have helped make the Temple of Love a delightful destination once again.

dramatic waterworks beneath it with five waterfalls and six cascades, were all restored. ("I know of nothing equaling the man-made romanticism of this spot in an American garden," Steve had written in 1995.) The Vista was cleared and replanted, so that the view down to the river was once more revealed (2017). The rock gardens near the Temple of Love were uncovered and reconfigured. The canals in the Walled Garden were dismantled and completely rebuilt with modern irrigation methods (2018). The lower entrance at the Old Croton Aqueduct and its connection to the ruined gatehouse were stabilized and restored (2019). More staff were hired. By 2019, there were seven gardeners working on the estate. Byrns had pulled off a miracle.

Remedial work on the pool and canals around the sphinxes was extensive.

The Legacy

After his death, Samuel Untermyer, who was a legendary figure both in the law and in public life, became a forgotten man. This was a personality who in 1928 was included in a book alongside Herbert Hoover, Jimmy Walker, Will Hays, and Theodore Roosevelt Jr. as a "Big Frog" in American history. In another book, published in 1942, titled *Famous in Their Twenties*, Untermyer again made the list, along with Lowell Thomas, Paul Robeson, Margaret Bourke-White, and other artists and celebrities. Yet not 10 years after his death, people looking at the names in these books no doubt recognized the others, but Samuel Untermyer? Who?

With the rescue of Untermyer's gardens, he himself has also been rescued. The lion of the courtroom who so long dominated New York's legal arena is now once more in the headlines. The record of his public-spirited career and reputation, long since buried, is now back in the world, where

The same area now is lush with water, fountains, and new plants that change with the seasons.

it belongs. As Steve Byrns put it, "Samuel Untermyer was consistently and progressively on the right side of history." As for the gardens which Untermyer created with such a splendid combination of personal satisfaction and cultural responsibility nearly 100 years ago, they have come back to life for the public to enjoy with the same delight that the famous lawyer once envisaged. In 2011, 5000 people visited the gardens. By 2017, that number had leaped to 75,000, a number that Untermyer himself could only have applauded.

The work of restoration continues. It may never be fully finished, but momentum is gathering. In January 2019, the Untermyer Gardens Conservancy was awarded a grant of $50,000 from the New York State Office of Parks, Recreation and Historic Preservation, to be matched by the Conservancy, for restoration of the newly named Persian Pool in the

The circular Temple of the Sky and adjacent pool, before improvements.

Walled Garden. (One wonders what Robert Moses would have thought about that!) These funds will lead to what the president of the Conservancy calls "our biggest project, the restoration of the mosaic-lined pool."

The swimming pool below the Temple of the Sky must be totally rebuilt and Bosworth's precious mosaics replaced. Plans are being made for a land swap with St. John's Hospital in order to restore the Color Gardens, replacing those dazzling flower beds that Untermyer so loved and the steps and pavilions that made Bosworth so proud. The Rose and Dahlia Gardens are also on the restoration list. And what about Chisholm's most fanciful creation for his master, the sundial? Definitely under consideration. The rock gardens, the carriage trails, the woods—the landscape is gradually being resurrected, stone by stone, plant by plant, seed by seed.

In 2013, Stephen Byrns wrote a mission statement, which read in part, "During the first half of the 20th century, the gardens were called America's most spectacular garden. Its centerpiece was the Walled Garden,

Renovation included reestablishing the lions' head fountains and repairing the mosaic art along the wall and floor of the pool.

the finest Indo-Persian-style garden in the Western Hemisphere. Another aspect of its significance is that it is based on the ancient concept of the Garden of Eden, which is shared by Judaism, Christianity, and Islam, and as such, is a multicultural symbol for Yonkers and the nation."

Samuel Untermyer could hardly have wished for a better epitaph.

FOLLOWING PAGES Stephen Byrns and the Untermyer Gardens Conservancy have brought back large portions of the gardens to showstopping, four-season beauty. Work continues to restore additional sections of the gardens.

Untermyer Gardens, 1940

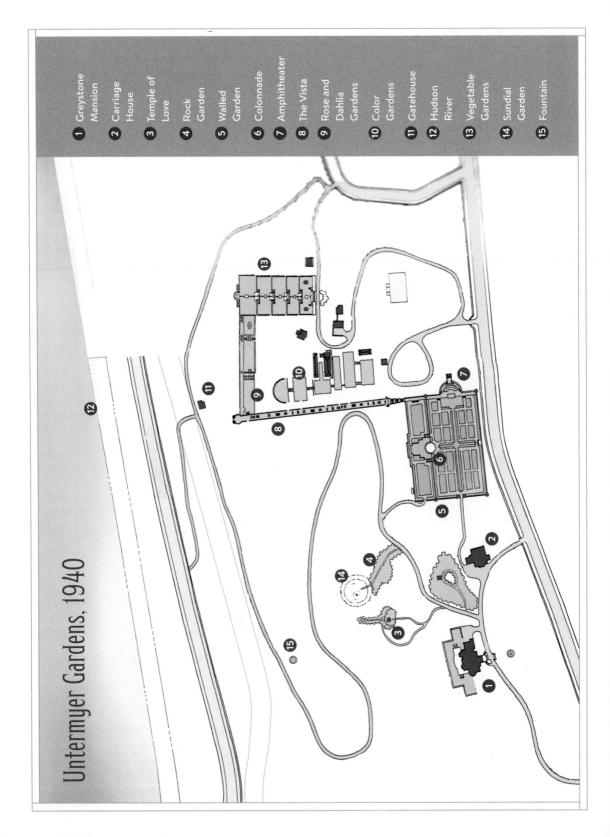

1 Greystone Mansion
2 Carriage House
3 Temple of Love
4 Rock Garden
5 Walled Garden
6 Colonnade
7 Amphitheater
8 The Vista
9 Rose and Dahlia Gardens
10 Color Gardens
11 Gatehouse
12 Hudson River
13 Vegetable Gardens
14 Sundial Garden
15 Fountain

Untermyer Gardens, 2018

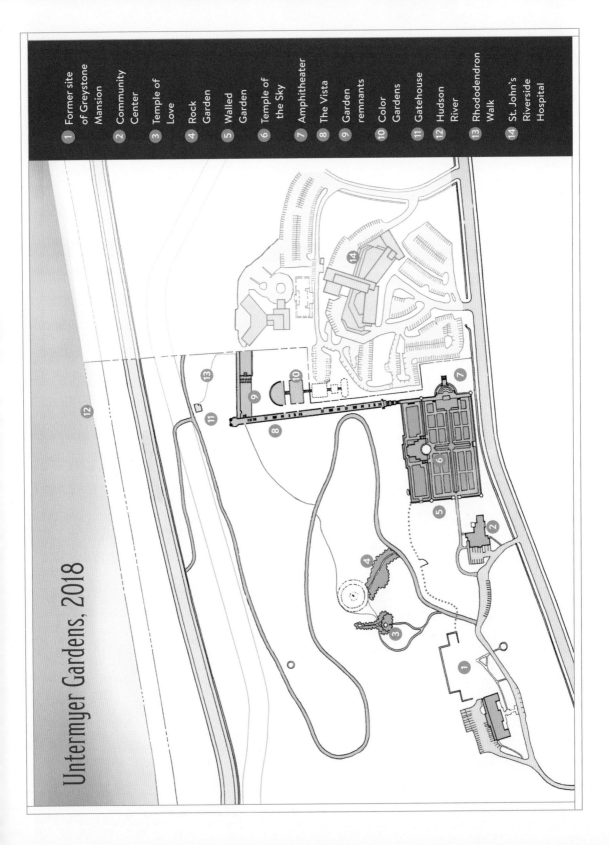

1. Former site of Greystone Mansion
2. Community Center
3. Temple of Love
4. Rock Garden
5. Walled Garden
6. Temple of the Sky
7. Amphitheater
8. The Vista
9. Garden remnants
10. Color Gardens
11. Gatehouse
12. Hudson River
13. Rhododendron Walk
14. St. John's Riverside Hospital

SELECT BIBLIOGRAPHY

Books and Reports

Griswold, Mac, and Eleanor Weller. 2000. *The Golden Age of American Gardens: Proud Owners, Private Estates, 1890–1940*. New York: Harry N. Abrams Inc.

Gross, Michael. 2009. *Rogues' Gallery: The Secret Story of the Lust, Lies, Greed, and Betrayals that Made the Metropolitan Museum of Art*. New York: Broadway Books.

Himber, Charlotte. 1942. *Famous in Their Twenties*. New York: Association Press.

Kroeger, Brooke. 2017. *The Suffragents: How Women Used Men to Get the Vote*. Albany, NY: State University of New York Press.

Michell, George, and Amit Pasricha. 2011. *Mughal Architecture & Gardens*. Suffolk, UK: Antique Collectors Club.

O'Donnell, Patricia M., et al. 1995. *Historic Landscape Report—Untermyer Park*. Yonkers, NY: City of Yonkers Department of Parks, Recreation & Conservation.

Pringle, Henry F. 1928. *Big Frogs*. New York: Vanguard Press.

Robinson, Barbara Paul. 2018. *Heroes of Horticulture: Americans Who Transformed the Landscape*. Boston: David R. Godine.

Seebohm, Caroline, and Curtice Taylor. 2015. *Rescuing Eden: Preserving America's Historic Gardens*. New York: The Monacelli Press.

Untermeyer, Jean Starr. 1965. *Private Collection*. New York: Knopf.

Vaught, Steve, and Tracy Conrad. 2015. *Einstein Dreamt Here: The Willows Historic Palm Springs Inn*. Palm Springs, CA: The Willows Historic Palm Springs Inn.

Warren, Charles D., Andrew Scott Dolkart, Alice Cooney Frelinghuysen, and Cynthia Mills. 2014. *Sylvan Cemetery: Architecture, Art and Landscape at Woodlawn*. New York: Avery Architectural & Fine Arts Library and The Woodlawn Conservancy.

Wharton, Edith. 1904. *Italian Villas and Their Gardens*. New York: The Century Co.

Yeats, John Butler. 1946. *Letters to His Son W.B. Yeats and Others, 1869–1922*. New York: E.P. Dutton and Company.

Articles

Deitz, Paula, "Placemaker: Stephen F. Byrns," *Site/Lines*, Volume X, Number 11, Spring 2015, pp. 21–23.

Hambidge, Gove, "Mr. Untermyer in His Enchanted Gardens," *Better Homes & Gardens*, February 1928, pp. 18–19, 128–130.

Hawkins, Richard. "Samuel Untermyer." In *Immigrant Entrepreneurship: German-American Business Biographies, 1720 to the Present, vol. 2*, edited by William J. Hausman. German Historical Institute. Last modified November 12, 2013. http://www.immigrantentrepreneurship.org/entry. php?rec = 181

Hellman, Geoffrey T., "The Boutonnieres of Mr. Untermyer," *The New Yorker*, May 18, 1940, pp. 54–65.

Hoar, Mary, "The Enchanted Gardens of Greystone." *The Yonkers Historian*, Spring 2010.

Jacobs, Quentin Snowden, "William Welles Bosworth: Major Works." Master's thesis, Columbia University, 1988.

Johnston, Alva, "Profiles: Little Giant—I." *The New Yorker*, May 17, 1930. pp. 29–32.

———, "Profiles: Little Giant—II." *The New Yorker*, May 24, 1930. pp. 24–27.

Ramirez, Jan Seidler, "Paul Manship and Samuel Untermyer: A Sculptor and His Patron." *The Westchester Historian*, Fall 1987, pp. 100–114.

Street, Pamela, "The Gardens at Greystone: The Grecian Glory of William Welles Bosworth." Course paper, Harvard University, 2009.

Warner, Ralph, "The Gardens at Greystone," *The Architectural Review*, December 1918, pp. 106–109.

ACKNOWLEDGMENTS

First of all, I must thank Stephen F. Byrns, president of the Untermyer Gardens Conservancy, for his tireless help in providing me with information about the history and rescue of the garden. He opened his files and archives, which are huge, and allowed me to pluck everything I wanted from them. He also pointed me to people who could help me, and subjects that I needed to research. The Untermyer Gardens are his life's work, so I could not have been luckier in having such a passionate and rigorous supporter of the book.

Untermyer family member Ann Carmel was very helpful and candid in telling me a great deal about her complicated lineage. Pamela Street told me stories, too, and lent me some photographs from her personal collection that were delightful additions to the book. (And thank you, Penelope Rowlands, for introducing Pamela to me!) The late Marian Heiskell's memories of her grandfather were particularly vivid.

Dr. Richard A. Hawkins was an invaluable and exceedingly generous source for me throughout my research. Professor Hawkins has written extensively on the legal and political aspects of Samuel Untermyer's life and work, and he responded patiently and quickly to all my endless questions about this, until now, mostly unknown lawyer.

Other people whom I'd like to single out for their generosity are Susan Olsen at Woodlawn Cemetery; Tracy Conrad at The Willows; Cynthia Altman at Kykuit; Elizabeth Shannon at Vizcaya; Ellen Roberts at the Norton Museum, Palm Beach; Pamela Casey at the Avery Library, Columbia University; and Stephanie Herdrich at the Metropolitan Museum of Art. Over several days, Kevin Proffitt made available to me enormously heavy volumes of Untermyer documents and clippings (which Alexis Horst sturdily carried to me) in the beautiful library of the Jacob Rader Marcus Center of the American Jewish Archives in Cincinnati, Ohio. I thank them all.

The following also helped me in various ways: Jamie Clark, Diana Kormos-Buchwald, Nortrud Spero, Joseph Koslowsky, Jack Staub, and Steven Vaught.

Églantine Pasquier, a Paris-based scholar who is working on a book about Welles Bosworth's career in France, shared all her relevant research with me, allowing me to develop a far more rounded picture of the architect than I had previously established. I am greatly indebted to her.

A special thank-you goes to Jennifer Stratton, a young digital genius who patiently sorted through the hundreds of images that arrived daily on my computer. Jenn saved me from a Luddite meltdown on more occasions than I care to count. How she did it I'll never know (nor do I wish to), but time and again she produced visual order out of chaos.

I must also mention here another essential contributor, Jessica Norman. Jessica is not only a gardener at the Untermyer Park and Gardens, but also a very talented photographer. Thus she was able to take photographs of the garden day and night, season by season, making it today one of the best-documented gardens in the United States. She helped make available to me the historic images from the Untermyer archives as well as her own brilliant photographic portfolio, and I am deeply grateful to her.

The cast at Timber Press who put together this book includes Tom Fischer, who first believed that Samuel Untermyer's story was worth telling; Sarah Milhollin, who turned the enormous archive of historic and contemporary photographs into acceptable formats for the book; Kim Thwaits and Sarah Crumb, inspired book designers, and Raphael Geroni, who came up with a brilliant cover; and the unflappable and always encouraging project editor, Julie Talbot.

The idea for this book sprang from an earlier book I wrote entitled *Rescuing Eden: Preserving America's Historic Gardens*, published by Monacelli in 2016. One of the stories featured in that book was about the Untermyer Gardens in Yonkers, and the person who brought it to me was the photographer of the book, Curtice Taylor. So it is thanks to Curtice's photographs that I first learned about Samuel Untermyer and his astonishing story, and realized what an interesting book it would make on its own. Thank you, Curtice.

PHOTOGRAPHY & ILLUSTRATION CREDITS

PHOTOGRAPHY

Alamy
Len Holsborg: page 8
Katharine Andriotis: page 12
Everett Collection Inc: page 36
BXF5AF: page 90 bottom
Len Holsborg: pages 122, 184, 193
The Picture Art Collection:
page 147
Randy Duchaine: page 192

American Jewish Archives: page 31

The Architectural Review, Vol. VII,
No.6, December, 1918 (scans courtesy
Washington State University Libraries,
Pullman): page 42

Courtesy of Brown University Library,
Brown Digital Repository: page 63

Getty Images
Rex Hardy Jr.: pages 39, 89
New York Daily News Archive:
page 51
Bettmann Archive: page 53
Michael Marquand: pages 164–165

© Bob Gruen: page 162

Courtesy of Harvard University,
Schlesinger Library on the History of
Women in America: page 23

Courtesy of Harvard Graduate School
of Design, Frances Loeb Library:
page 72

Hudson River Museum: pages 44, 125,
133, 136, 153, 157

iStockphoto
seven75: page 67
jonnysek: page 107
JNevitt: page 112

Courtesy of William G. Kleindienst, mayor of Palm Springs, California, 1995–2005: pages 49, 55

Courtesy of the Library of Congress: pages 10, 16, 26, 28, 29, 34, 41, 61, 64, 65, 66, 68, 69, 94, 127, 140, 151

Courtesy of the Metropolitan Museum of Art: pages 40, 156

Courtesy of the National Gallery of Art Library, Department of Image Collections, Parke-Bernet Archive: page 129

© New-York Historical Society: page 19

Jessica Norman: pages 2–3, 5, 6–7, 14, 43, 45, 58, 70, 73, 74, 75, 76–77, 83, 85, 92, 98, 105, 117, 118, 138, 142, 145, 154, 169, 174, 177, 178, 179, 181, 183, 186–187 all, 189, 190, 191, 194–195, 196–197, 198–199, 200–201

Caroline Seebohm: pages 170, 171

Shutterstock
John Arehart: page 80
Marcio Jose Bastos Silva: page 95

Courtesy of the Smithsonian Institution, Archives of American Art: page 87

Courtesy of the Smithsonian Institution, Archives of American Gardens, Untermyer Family Slide Collection, Samuel Untermyer II: pages 104, 109, 116, 120, 121

Courtesy of Pamela Street: pages 20, 131

Courtesy of © Curtice Taylor: page 188

Courtesy of the Untermyer family archive: page 149

Courtesy of the Untermyer Gardens Conservancy, McGuirk Collection: pages 82, 101, 106, 135

Courtesy of the Untermyer Gardens Conservancy, Historic Photos Collection: pages 103, 159, 160, 166

Westchester County Historical Society: page 38

Wikimedia Commons
Released into the Public Domain
photographer unknown: page 32
Hugo Rudolphy, page 90 top
Used under a Creative Common Attribution 3.0 Unported license, JamesPFisherIII: page 47

ILLUSTRATION

Westchester County Archives: pages 96–97

Courtesy of the Untermyer Gardens Conservancy: pages 202–203

INDEX